Modern

Public

Gardens

Modern

REUBEN M. RAINEY
JC MILLER

Public

ROBERT ROYSTON AND

Gardens

THE SUBURBAN PARK

Berkeley/Design/Books #3

WILLIAM STOUT
PUBLISHERS
SAN FRANCISCO

This book was published with the assistance of
The Getty Foundation,
the Graham Foundation for Advanced Studies
in the Fine Arts,
and Royston Hanamoto Alley & Abey

Published in cooperation with the
College of Environmental Design,
University of California, Berkeley

Berkeley/Design/Books promote historical and critical
scholarship on subjects drawn from the Environmental
Design Archives at the University of California, Berkeley.
One of the nation's premier design archives, its collections
hold graphic materials, written documents, and personal
papers concerning American and foreign architecture,
landscape architecture, and planning.

Marc Treib, Series Editor
Waverly Lowell, Archives Curator

ISBN 0-9746214-2-0

Library of Congress Control Number 2006927906

Designed by Marc Treib

Published by
William Stout Publishers
530 Greenwich Street
San Francisco, California 94133
www.stoutbooks.com

Printed in China

For Asa Hanamoto, Kaz Alley, Pat Carlisle,
Harold Kobayashi, and Robert Royston

Introduction

In late 1944 off the coast of the Gilbert Islands, Navy First Lieutenant Robert N. Royston was on duty aboard the attack transport USN *Pondera*. In the rare moments his demanding duties allowed, he sketched and modeled imaginary residences and gardens, ideal visions of form and space he hoped to create when peace returned. Commanding landing craft that ferried assault troops to the bloody atolls of the South Pacific, he experienced firsthand the horrific suffering of war. His reverie of professional work in postwar America—an America freed from the lingering effects of the Great Depression and the privations of four years of war—was a welcome escape from carnage to creativity (figure 1).

The young lieutenant's designs, which attracted the attention of his shipmates, were not the fantasies of a novice. They were grounded in the rigorous curriculum of landscape architectural studies at the University of California, Berkeley, and tested in the office of one of the nation's most gifted landscape architects, Thomas D. Church, where he had worked for two years before enlisting in the Navy in 1942.

After logging about 150,000 miles at sea, Royston returned to the San Francisco Bay Area in 1945 to resume a career in landscape architecture that would span half a century and produce projects ranging from residential

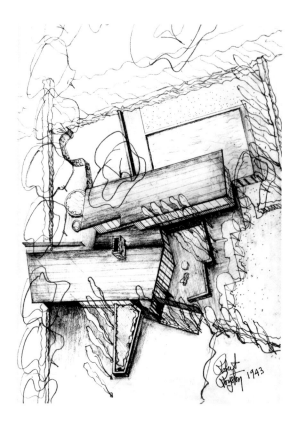

1. ROYSTON'S STUDY SKETCH FOR A POSTWAR HOME CLOSELY INTEGRATED WITH ITS SITE, DRAWN ABOARD SHIP WHILE OFF DUTY, 1943. [ENVIRONMENTAL DESIGN ARCHIVES, UNIVERSITY OF CALIFORNIA, BERKELEY (HEREAFTER EDA, UCB)]

gardens to new towns. He credits those early shipboard exercises, honed in the chaos of war, as fundamental to his development and important throughout his career.

Among Royston's most important achievements are his early suburban park projects. Most were in the Bay Area and constructed from 1945 to 1965. During this twenty-year period Royston and his professional partners created a series of suburban parks of varying scale that pioneered new directions in American park design. These projects were innovative in their spatial organization, design details, and materials, creatively reshaping American park design traditions to meet the unprecedented needs of postwar suburban expansion. They attracted national attention in design periodicals and earned numerous design awards from the American Society of Landscape Architects, including a prestigious Award Of Honor.

Royston did not view these parks as isolated entities: rather, he envisioned them as a system of interconnected recreational spaces that he called a "landscape matrix." Together with other kinds of public spaces, they would bring order and amenity to rapidly developing suburbs that often suffered for lack of intelligent planning. He recognized that the design of suburbs would frame much of his professional career, and he welcomed the challenges they presented.

Unlike several critics who viewed the suburbs as stultifying environments that degraded their inhabitants, he saw the potential for vibrant and engaging places, where enlightened site planning would encourage shared community values.[1] For Royston parks were a major part of that vision (figure 2).

In designing these parks Royston employed the rich spatial definition and fresh biomorphic and cubist forms he had experimented with on shipboard and implemented in his residential gardens in the late 1940s and early 1950s. The result was a series of suburban parks with dynamic interlocking spaces zoned for diverse recreational uses catering to a wide range of age groups. These parks possessed a welcoming familiarity. Many of their elements—pergolas, paving patterns, picnic nooks—were similar in form and materials to those found in the private gardens of their suburban users (figure 3). Indeed Royston called his early parks "public gardens" and designed them to bring neighborhoods together for group recreational activities and civic celebrations to promote that often elusive goal of urban planning, a sense of community.

While Royston has devoted considerable attention to park design throughout his fifty-five-year career, it was the suburban parks of the first two decades that established

2. CENTRAL PARK, SANTA CLARA, 1960-75. [JC MILLER, 2004]

3. *(OPPOSITE PAGE)* BOWERS PARK, SANTA CLARA, 1960. THIS PERGOLA IS SIMILAR TO THOSE ROYSTON DESIGNED FOR RESIDENTIAL GARDENS. [REUBEN RAINEY, 2004]

the conceptual framework for much of his later park work. Thus this period merits special attention. Many of these parks are still in use today. For the most part, they have not been altered substantially although they may have suffered from low maintenance before being restored. Their survival is not related to meager municipal budgets or nostalgia for the design expressions of the 1950s. Most of them are located in highly affluent communities, such as Palo Alto and Santa Clara, nurtured by the bounty of the semiconductor industry and prestigious research universities. If they so desired, these communities could demolish these parks and construct new ones. Instead, their vocal and politically active citizens have, with few exceptions, insisted that Royston's parks be maintained or restored according to the original designs. Why? Because they know from experience these parks enrich their lives and the lives of their families, friends, and neighbors. In the late 1990s, schoolchildren appeared before Palo Alto's city council to request that Mitchell Park, which had suffered from poor maintenance, be repaired and rebuilt to substantially its original form.[2] Many older citizens supported the request based on their vivid childhood memories, and council members granted it. Such parks, many of which have endured for half a century—amid the cacophony of our

postindustrial age, so enamored of novelty and consumption—invite a closer look.

Our study begins with a brief biography and a discussion of the design climate in the Bay Area in the years immediately following World War II. Next we examine the theory that informed Royston's park work and describe his design process, which includes an account of how he collaborated with park and recreation officials. Finally, to illustrate the variety of form, scale, and function in his designs, we analyze representative suburban parks from this early period. This series of projects begins with his park for Ladera Cooperative Housing Project of 1946 and ends with his Santa Clara Civic Center Park of 1964. Royston himself considers the case studies we have focused on to be the most important of his earlier park designs, and we agree with his assessment. After a discussion of the present condition of several of the featured parks, we conclude with suggestions of how Royston's approach to park design can contribute to current attempts to address the question, "What kind of parks should we provide for twenty-first century cities and suburbs?" We will make the case that at the core of that contribution is Royston's vision of a system of interconnected "public gardens" whose design is carefully based on human needs

and the protection and enhancement of the natural environment—places to experience the challenges of competitive team sport, quiet encounters with nature's restorative power, the joy of artistic creativity, the discovery of the natural world, and the simple pleasures of informal neighborhood events: places that foster strong community bonds and create an environment that both educates and delights.

We have based this study on a wide variety of resources: the extensive materials in the Environmental Design Archives of the University of California, Berkeley; office records of Royston Hanamoto Alley & Abey in Mill Valley; and the libraries of Stanford University and the College of Environmental Design at the University of California, Berkeley. We also conducted many personal interviews with Robert Royston between 2002 and 2004 and consulted the materials in his personal collection. In addition, we accompanied him on visits to several of the works discussed: The Rod and Gun Club (Point Richmond), Bowden and Mitchell Parks (Palo Alto), and Central Park and Civic Center Park (Santa Clara). We also conducted on-site studies of eight additional Royston parks of varying scale and function on the San Francisco peninsula. Finally, we consulted a brief 1950 documentary film on Mitchell Park and the tape of a television interview with Robert Royston conducted in 2002.

Acknowledgments

The staff of the Environmental Design Archives of the University of California, Berkeley, has provided indispensable assistance with the Royston/RHAA Collection. Curator Waverly Lowell and Assistant Curator Carrie McDade have led us to many riches in this valuable collection. The entire staff, including Betsy Frederick-Rothwell, MacKenzie Bennett, April Hesik, and Meredith Hall, have been of considerable help.

Robert Royston provided autobiographical reflections, slides, and drawings of his work from his personal collection and analysis of his suburban parks. He patiently responded to our relentless questioning and graced us with his presence on several field trips. He also critiqued our manuscript and offered many helpful suggestions.

Marc Treib, with his characteristic vision and grasp of salient issues, offered us the opportunity to contribute this study to the Berkeley/Design/Books Series sponsored by the University of California, Berkeley's College of Environmental Design. Through the years, he has been a colleague on our research expeditions into the far reaches of landscape architecture. His sharp editorial eye and disdain for jargon have been of great value, as have his talents as a book designer.

Robert Royston's firm, Royston Hanamoto Alley & Abey, provided access to resources on the firm's early projects, and we are grateful to them for preserving these materials, some of which are a half century old. Future researchers will also benefit from their foresight in preserving valuable historical documents.

Peter Burgess, Lilla Burgess, and Rebecca Frischkorn read earlier drafts and offered useful suggestions. Our text has benefited from the early critical readings given it by Lance Neckar and Tom Martinson. Paul Groth, Dell Upton, and William Morrish shared their considerable knowledge of source materials dealing with the history of the San Francisco Bay Area. Sue Rainey has been a constant and inspiring support and has brought her skills as an editor and critic to bear on the manuscript. Our chief editor, Karen Madsen, has been outstanding, especially her nuanced suggestions for clarity and succinctness. Finally, we thank William Stout for supporting this work and enabling it to include the graphic documentation that Royston's achievements deserve. Of course, as authors, we take full responsibility for our interpretations and any errors of fact that may occur.

Reuben M. Rainey
Charlottesville, Virginia

JC Miller
Point Richmond, California

CHAPTER ONE

Early Years
and Education

Robert Norman Royston spent his childhood and teenage years amidst the functional geometry of agricultural land and engaged in the steady work routine of life on a ranch.[3] He was born on April 25, 1918, in San Francisco. When he was six years old, his family moved from Marin County to the Santa Clara Valley after his father, Walter Cyril, a mechanical and electrical engineer, retired in his mid-forties. Walter, wishing to remain active, purchased a twenty-acre walnut ranch near the small town of Morgan Hill. Here Royston and his older brother and younger sister helped Walter and their mother, Doris, with the daily work (figure 4). A rural upbringing was characteristic of many landscape architects of the nineteenth and twentieth centuries, among them Jens Jensen and Royston's mentor at the University of California, Berkeley, H. Leland Vaughan. Close contact early in life with the seasonal cycles—including plant growth from seedtime to harvest—was excellent preparation for a profession centered on accommodating human needs with natural processes.

The Santa Clara Valley of Royston's youth was a tapestry of orchards, livestock farms, and quiet market towns such as Gilroy and San Martin. The valley's rich alluvial soil and high water table suited it exceptionally well for agriculture, and the Coastal Mountains framing it on the east and west added a touch of scenic beauty. Today, densely packed suburbs and their companion malls and shopping centers fed by Highway 101 creep across the valley, obliterating the rural idyll of Royston's childhood. They are clones of their older siblings to the north in the East Bay or San Francisco peninsula, those suburbs of the 1950s and 60s to which he sought to bring order and amenity through his park designs and planned residential developments.

Young Royston's routine of seasonal chores on the walnut ranch—planting, irrigating, picking, and drying—as well as his firsthand knowledge of its no-nonsense, functional site plan, channeled some precocious interests in the direction of gardening and city planning. At the age of eight, on his own initiative, he planted and tended a small vegetable garden and sold its produce to his mother. This early venture in gardening was followed by the creation of an elaborate model for an ideal city. When he was ten, a family trip to Santa Barbara acquainted him with the elegance and order of that city and the beauty of its south-facing oceanfront framed by mountains. Upon returning home Royston made a model that was far from the typical pile of blocks on the playroom floor. The city's buildings were constructed of compressed soil and were sited

4. ROYSTON FARM, SANTA CLARA VALLEY, EARLY 1930s. WALNUTS ARE DRYING ON THE RACKS. [PERSONAL PAPERS OF ROBERT ROYSTON. (HEREAFTER PPRR)]

outdoors on a large twenty-by-forty-foot plot. Its streets were on a grid pattern with stop signs and traffic lights at each intersection, and it included shopping centers, residential areas, and an airport. Attentive to context, young Royston surrounded his city with mountains and an oceanfront. No one had suggested that he create such a model; he simply did it of his own accord, an obvious portent of his future vocation. Reflecting on the model today, Royston laughs and remarks that he built it not only because he was fascinated by what he had seen, but because "it was the first time I realized there were cities out there other than Morgan Hill."

Outdoor activities were a large part of his routine. He especially enjoyed hunting the ground squirrels, rabbits, and other "pests" that threatened the family's crops. Thus, his early view of "nature" was not that of the urban romantic but of the farmer who knew firsthand its bounty and its pitfalls.

During his years at Morgan Hill High School, Royston discovered additional interests. He excelled in art classes and his teachers encouraged him to develop his talent. He was also gifted in basketball and track and enjoyed participating in dramatic performances. One teacher who recognized his verbal skills and physical grace advised, "Robert, you should either be a lawyer or a ballet dancer."[4]

While engaging in the typical senior-year rite of choosing a college, Royston perused the catalog of the University of California, Berkeley, and came upon a major listed in the College of Agriculture entitled "Landscape Design." Its course requirements seemed to describe a discipline that drew together Royston's wide range of interests in drawing, theater, agriculture, and the outdoors. A trip to Berkeley for an interview with the chair of the program, John W. Gregg, confirmed Royston's expectations. He applied and was accepted. Royston vividly recalls Gregg's succinct, rapid-fire questions during the hour-long interview.

Did I enjoy drawing? Yes. Did I like music? Yes. Did I like theater? Yes. Did I like nature? Yes. Was I a good student? Yes. At the end of the interview, Gregg said [something] to the effect that I would enjoy a career in Landscape Architecture and he would accept me in the department.[5]

Royston's college years were framed by the Great Depression and World War II. Both the Bay Area and the profession of landscape architecture were in a state of transition.[6] The Bay Area's economy had been severely damaged by the Depression: No longer was San Francisco the West Coast's major center of shipping and industry, having been surpassed by Los Angeles. The rapid suburban growth, especially of the East Bay, which had been fueled by the automobile and post-World War I prosperity, had slowed substantially. Royston, like many students during this time of scarcity, worked his way through college with odd jobs for the Division of Landscape Design and on Saturdays in the office of Thomas Church. In the summer of 1937 he gained valuable experience as a construction laborer for Watsonville landscape architect Arthur Hyde. The following summer he worked in Church's office, constructing gardens for residences on the San Francisco peninsula. In the little spare time he could afford, he joined the university's drama group and did some summer stock performances with the Ross Players in Marin County.[7] Later, Royston would draw upon his experience in theater to hone his presentation skills.

The profession Royston had chosen was experiencing a major shift in response to the ever-increasing impact of the automobile on urban form, the staggering economic disaster of the Great Depression, and the public works programs of President Franklin Roosevelt's New Deal. The lucrative commissions for large residential estate gardens that sustained so many offices in the early century had vanished nearly as rapidly as the value of Wall Street stocks. The advent of income taxes and changing ideas of how to display one's wealth—away from large landed estates—meant

such work would never regain its former volume and scale, although smaller-scale residential site planning would undergo something of a recovery in the post-World War II period, especially in California. To avoid economic disaster, most offices in California and elsewhere turned to commissions in the public sector. There were of course exceptions like Thomas Church, who continued working on single-family residences while his income was supplemented by a few government-funded, larger-scale housing projects. The alphabet agencies of the New Deal, especially the Civilian Conservation Corps and the greatly expanded National Park Service, provided much-needed new work. In addition, government funding of state park systems, farm labor camps, low-cost urban housing, and parkway construction furnished additional employment.

By the late 1930s, 600 landscape architects were employed by the National Park Service, and more than half of the 450 members of the American Society of Landscape Architects were working for state and federal agencies.[8] This was a period of enormous public works, northern California's Contra Costa Canal and Mokelumne River projects and the San Francisco-Oakland Bay and Golden Gate bridges among them. For landscape architects in the

Bay Area, park projects such as Aquatic Park, Mount Diablo State Park, and the large East Bay Regional Park District offered welcome employment. Not only were project types changing but younger professionals like Garrett Eckbo, Dan Kiley, and James Rose were creating new design vocabularies. These were influenced by forms new to the twentieth-century: the layered spaces of Mies van der Rohe's Barcelona Pavilion, French experiments in garden design, and biomorphic, constructivist, and cubist painting and sculpture. Like most such periods of transition, these years exhibited a complex blend of exhilarating novelty and daunting ambiguity. It was a good time to be a student of landscape architecture, urban design, and community planning.

Royston's ambitions were well served by the University of California, Berkeley's Division of Landscape Design, which had been established in the School of Agriculture in 1913. (In the early twentieth century, it was typical of land grant universities to locate landscape design programs in the agriculture schools.) While the program was no cauldron of avant-garde ideas, it did possess several strengths. The four-year undergraduate degree offered a sound foundation in the liberal arts and sciences, which helped students gain a critical perspective on their design work. The tech-

nical curriculum was strong and the program included an important interdisciplinary dimension. In addition to their landscape design studies students were required to complete twenty-seven units in studio art and architecture, six in botany, and three in civil engineering. Like most such programs of its day, it was small, consisting of three full-time professors and about thirty students. (Nine students graduated in Royston's class in 1940.) It was one of ten programs in the U.S. that were granted an "A" ranking by the American Society of Landscape Architects, its highest designation based on the quality of the faculty, student body, facilities, and resources.[9] Royston remembers it as a supportive academic community with high morale and energy, presided over by a capable faculty whose teaching was shaped by their strong involvement in professional practice. And even though they themselves did not share them, they allowed students to explore some of the more innovative design approaches advocated by Christopher Tunnard, James Rose, Dan Kiley, and Garrett Eckbo in the late 1930s. Thus professors avoided indoctrinating students with design dogma and encouraged them to develop and critique their own ideas. The heart of this curriculum consisted of three full years of design studio, one year of history, one year of construction, two years of planting design, and a summer field course that included tours of landscape architectural firms and important sites in California.[10] Royston thrived in this tolerant yet intense academic community.

The teacher who most influenced Royston was H. Leland Vaughan. Vaughan was the youngest of the three faculty members and had taught in the program since 1930. He was a graduate of Ohio State's program in landscape design, where Thomas Church had been his teacher. Impressed with his abilities, Church had recommended him for a position at Berkeley. Garrett Eckbo (class of 1935) remembers Vaughan as a "young maverick" and gifted teacher who encouraged his students "to keep an open mind and to form their own opinion."[11] Vaughan quickly established ties between local practitioners and Berkeley's program. His close relationship with Thomas Church enabled him to help Royston find part-time work in Church's office, where experiments with a fresh design vocabulary had begun, influenced by some of the more avant-garde ideas current at the time. Vaughan's ideas contrasted sharply with those of the program's other two full-time professors, division chair John Gregg and Harry Shepherd, both rooted in the traditional Beaux-Arts school of landscape architecture, with its eclectic synthesis of eighteenth-century English landscape design traditions and those of the Italian Renaissance and seventeenth-century France. This approach was typical of most design programs in the United States and had been codified in Henry Hubbard and Theodore Kimball's classic, *An Introduction to the Study of Landscape Design*, first published in 1917. Vaughan taught junior-year studio, construction, and history. In his history courses he cautioned against using the work of the past as a grab bag of stylistic solutions. Rather, he advocated history as a means of understanding the values embodied in works of the past. By studying the designs of previous eras, a student would become aware of the values expressed in his or her own work and how it might address the needs of twentieth-century American society. Royston vividly recalls Vaughan's approach to teaching:

He wasn't a teacher who was long on theory or with deep convictions on the natural evolution of design. He had a way of remaining silent, and it was his silence that taught me the most. He would come and look at my drawings and he just sort of grunted and that meant "keep going" or if he started to talk about it then he'd just take you a little bit farther on something. Usually if he said nothing he was approving.[12]

In addition to Vaughan, major influences on young Royston were the required courses in studio art, which centered mostly on drawing and graphic design. Under the tutelage of John Haley he created abstract, geometric compositions in black and white, which taught him basic design principles. Earl Loran introduced him to many of the great paintings of Western tradition and taught him various methods of design analysis. Margaret Peterson instructed him in drawing and critiqued his studio work in landscape architecture, giving Royston a valuable interdisciplinary perspective. These experiences developed Royston's strong conviction—which he adhered to throughout his long career—that landscape architectural design flourishes when it is in close dialogue with kindred arts (figure 5).[13]

Under Vaughan's tolerant mentorship in his studio work and through his part-time work in the office of Church, Royston began to develop his own approach, which was deeply influenced by biomorphic and cubist forms as well as spatial concepts in the architecture of Le Corbusier and Mies van der Rohe. He studied Picasso's analytical cubist paintings and sculpture and attended numerous exhibitions of modern art in the Bay Area. He read with interest the essays co-authored by Dan Kiley, James Rose, and his future professional partner Garrett Eckbo in *Pencil Points*, *Architectural Record*, and other periodicals.[14] He found himself in complete sympathy with their call for a new design perspective and methodology that would address the specific needs of twentieth-century society. Some of the other catalysts for the development of his design theory were published illustrations of Thomas Church's gardens in popular magazines such as *Sunset* and *Better Homes and Gardens*—particularly influential was an illustration of Church's Jerd Sullivan Garden of 1935 (figure 6). Another important influence was the 1937 exhibition "Contemporary Landscape Architecture" at the San Francisco Museum of Art. The brief but probing essays in the exhibition catalog by Richard Neutra, Henry-Russell Hitchcock Jr., and Fletcher Steele refined Royston's knowledge of landscape architectural modernism.[15] A bit later two small gardens by Thomas Church tucked away in a corner of the Golden Gate exhibition grounds displayed innovative forms and use of materials that deeply impressed Royston. The composition of Kandinsky's paintings with their charged juxtapositions of sweeping arcs and converging diagonals also engaged his attention.[16]

By the late 1930s the garden as a laboratory for experimentation had recovered somewhat from its post-Depression decline, at least in California, with its strong residential traditions of outdoor living and the close interconnection

of house and garden. However, the majority of these gardens were at a considerably smaller scale than the estate gardens of the pre-Depression years. Vaughan had observed in the Berkeley student publication *Axis* in the late 1930s: "The interest is centering more and more on the design of the garden as a whole and the civilization of the garden space as a comfortable and efficient unit of the residence."[17] Vaughan's remarks prophesied Royston's early professional career. After his graduation in 1940 Royston would experiment in the laboratory of garden design as a full-time employee of Thomas Church and would continue to develop new ideas on residential site planning in his own firm and as a teacher in the years following World War II.

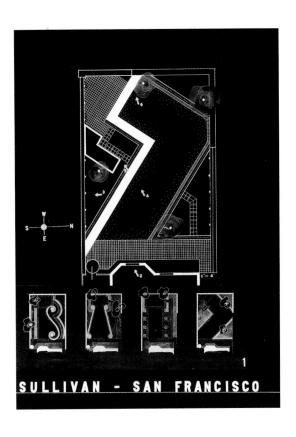

5. *(OPPOSITE PAGE)* A RESIDENTIAL SITE PLAN PREPARED BY ROYSTON AS A STUDENT AT BERKELEY BEFORE HIS DISCOVERY OF BIOMORPHIC AND CUBIST FORMS, 1938. [EDA, UCB]

6. SULLIVAN GARDEN, SAN FRANCISCO, 1935. ILLUSTRATIVE MODEL PREPARED BY ROYSTON FOR AN EXHIBITION WHILE WORKING IN THE OFFICE OF THOMAS CHURCH. [EDA, UCB]

CHAPTER TWO

First Professional Work and War Experience, 1940–1945

With Hitler's armies devastating Europe and Japan's imperialist ambitions growing ever stronger in the Far East, 1940 was a time of uncertainty for a young man of twenty-two embarking on a career. The local economy had recovered to some extent, which improved the job market for landscape architects. In the period immediately preceding the war, over fifty percent were still employed by federal and state governments. Royston chose the route of private practice, serving a valuable apprenticeship in Church's office between his graduation and enlistment in the Navy in 1942. He began work in the small, three-person office at an auspicious time. Not only was Church beginning to experiment with new forms in his residential work, he also undertook innovative large-scale housing projects supported by government funding.

Church also collaborated with architects of a more modernist persuasion, such as John Funk, who had recently completed the Heckendorf house in Modesto, and William Wurster, who was just beginning work on the Schuckl building in Sunnyvale while continuing to design a series of residences. These individuals and others, such as Joseph Stein, were to become important colleagues in Royston's postwar professional practice, which thrived in the lively atmosphere of collaboration

characteristic of Bay Area architects, landscape architects, and engineers during the
1930s and early 1940s, and continuing in the
postwar years. Royston also joined Telesis,
an informal group of designers and planners
concerned with the environmental problems
of the San Francisco Bay Area. There he first
met his future professional partner and friend
Garrett Eckbo.[18]

Shortly after Royston entered the office, Church
collaborated with William Wurster and Harry
A. Thomson on Valencia Gardens, a public
housing project funded by the United States
Housing Authority (figure 7). The next major
housing project was for Potrero Hill; Royston
supervised the installation of the planting
plan, which required a crew of twenty using
jackhammers to make planting holes in the
site's solid bedrock. Shortly thereafter Church
received the commission to plan Park Merced,
a 200-acre housing project on the western
edge of San Francisco, for the Metropolitan
Insurance Company. Royston detailed plans
for the housing blocks' many inner courtyards,
working in close collaboration with Douglas
Baylis and his college mentor Leland Vaughan.[19]
The plan's clear separation of pedestrian and
automobile circulation influenced the site-
planning principles Royston applied in his
later career, especially in suburban parks

7. *(OPPOSITE PAGE)* VALENCIA GARDENS PUBLIC HOUSING, SAN FRANCISCO, 1939–1943. WILLIAM WURSTER, HARRY THOMAS, JR., ARCHITECTS. THE RAISED TURF ISLANDS PROTECT THE LAWNS FROM PEDESTRIAN AND BICYCLE TRAFFIC AND PROVIDE SEATING. [ROGER STURTEVANT, EDA, UCB]

8. ROBERT ROYSTON, FIRST LIEUTENANT, USN *PONDERA*, 1944. [PPRR]

such as Mitchell Park and Santa Clara's Central Park. The issues posed by these large-scale urban projects also reinforced Royston's interest in city planning.[20]

Royston resigned from the Church office in 1942 to enlist for officer training in the United States Navy (figure 8). He recalls with gratitude his brief years in the Church office:

Our work consisted mostly of gardens, varying in size usually from one to five acres. It was a great training ground…Those years mark a special place in my memory. Tommy [Church] had a friendliness toward life in general, a way of enjoying his profession that fostered an office ambiance conducive to creativity. His design was quiet and sure, a transitionist in detail and space, Victorian and yet modern.[21]

Most of Royston's war years were spent amid the horror of the carnage surrounding him, with brief moments of respite centering on his shipboard design exercises:

I wanted to go. I felt I should go to help stop Hitler…They were days of terror really. You just couldn't understand what was going on…It was a horrible experience to be with the dead and dying and the fact that you [the U.S. forces] had done it…We had a lot of dead people aboard ship, they died going back to Pearl [Harbor]. It is what you see, hear, smell and touch in death that turns the mind and I was no exception…I can still remember those kinds of things…you grew up fast.[22]

At first Ensign Royston ferried marines to the beaches under fire. Upon being promoted to First Lieutenant he was put in charge of repairing and loading the USN *Pondera*, his attack transport. It was during this time that he found the spare moments to pursue his imaginary projects, working primarily with scrap materials. He also designed small pieces of jewelry for his wife Evelyn Dunwoodie, whom he had married in 1941 (figures 9a, 9b). After two-and-a-half years at sea, in combat operations from Alaska to the South Pacific, Royston returned to the Bay Area to resume his profession. He recalls, "When I sailed through the Golden Gate I wasn't going anywhere ever again. Ever! I mean it took me fifteen years to make a major trip."

Once back in San Francisco, Royston was confronted with a difficult decision. Church apparently assumed he would resume his old position but had not issued a particularly strong invitation. Garrett Eckbo, whose

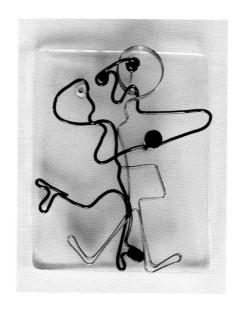

9A, 9B. JEWELRY FABRICATED BY ROYSTON FROM SCRAP MATERIAL WHILE ONBOARD SHIP IN THE PACIFIC. THE LAYERED COMPOSITIONS, STRONG SENSE OF LINE, AND ASYMMETRICAL POLYGONS ANTICIPATE THE RESIDENTIAL GARDEN PLANS THAT HE WOULD DESIGN LATER IN THE 1940s. [REUBEN RAINEY, 2005]

innovative work he admired and who through Telesis had become his close friend before the war, strongly urged him to join in partnership with him and landscape architect Edward Williams. Eckbo's strong social ethic combined with a fresh design persuasion similar to the one Royston was developing made him an ideal partner (figure 10). It was simply too great an opportunity to refuse, and in 1945 the firm of Eckbo, Royston and Williams opened offices in San Francisco and two years later in Los Angeles. Establishing dual offices allowed the partners to extend their practice over a wider geographical area. Royston and Williams headed the San Francisco office, Eckbo the one in Los Angeles. Williams had his own set of clients and was primarily responsible for the business affairs of the San Francisco office. To maintain their ties of friendship and to keep informed of current projects, the partners met in Los Angeles on a regular basis (figure 11).[23]

The issue of authorship often arises when individuals work as partners in the same office. In this case, the San Francisco office operated almost entirely on its own and in the firm's early days was responsible for most of the projects located in the Bay Area. The partners rarely exchanged specific ideas or critiqued each other's work.[24] During this period, which lasted until 1958, Royston designed some of his most innovative and successful parks as well as a wide range of other types of commissions, from private residential gardens to planned suburban communities. Possessing an abundance of energy, he also embarked on a full-time academic career while leading the San Francisco office (figure 12).

In 1947 Royston began teaching at Berkeley in the Division of Landscape Design, which still remained in the School of Agriculture. (In 1949 the name was changed to Landscape Architecture and the program was elevated in status to a department. In 1959 the department relocated in the newly formed College of Environmental Design.) Refusing to sign the loyalty oath demanded by California at the height of the McCarthy era, he resigned his assistant professor's position in 1951. During his tenure at Berkeley, Royston experimented with new ideas in his studios in city planning and enriched his teaching by sharing his professional experience with his students, many of whom were degree candidates in architecture (figures 13, 14). Also, in the early days of the San Francisco office Royston's academic salary helped keep the firm solvent. After leaving Berkeley he taught in the planning program at Stanford University for a brief

period. Throughout his professional career he maintained close ties to academia, serving as instructor or guest lecturer in departments of architecture and landscape architecture at twenty-four universities. This long association gave him a critical perspective on his work as well as a valuable source of fresh ideas.[25]

In 1958 Royston amicably parted from Eckbo and Williams and created a new firm with former Eckbo, Royston and Williams employees Asa Hanamoto and David Mayes, both of whom had been his students at the University of California.[26] Royston, Hanamoto, and Mayes, first based in San Francisco and later in Mill Valley, developed into Royston Hanamoto Alley & Abey, which is still active after forty- six years in its Mill Valley location (figure 15). The firm has undertaken a wide range of projects in the United States, Venezuela, Chile, Mexico, Canada, Singapore, and Malaysia and received over seventy design awards. These projects include private gardens, parkways, zoos, urban plazas, office parks, regional land-use plans, parks, campus plans, cemeteries, and new towns—the broad spectrum typical of the large corporate offices that developed during the late 1960s (figure 16). (Royston is now officially retired but remains active as a consultant.)

10. *(OPPOSITE PAGE ABOVE)* ROYSTON AND GARRETT ECKBO ON A TRIP TO CANADA, 1949. [EVELYN ROYSTON, EDA, UCB]

11. *(OPPOSITE PAGE BELOW)* THE PRINCIPALS OF ECKBO, ROYSTON AND WILLIAMS. FROM THE LEFT: GARRETT ECKBO, FRANCIS DEAN, EDWARD WILLIAMS, AND ROBERT ROYSTON. NO DATE, [ROYSTON HANAMOTO ALLEY & ABBEY ARCHIVES (HEREAFTER RHAA)]

12. APPERT GARDEN #2, ATHERTON, EARLY 1950s. PRIVATE RESIDENTIAL GARDENS WERE A MAINSTAY OF ROYSTON'S EARLY PROFESSIONAL PRACTICE. AN EARLY CONCEPT DRAWING FOR THIS GARDEN CAN BE SEEN IN FIGURE 32. [RHAA]

Working in his newly established partnership in the late 1950s and early 1960s, Royston continued his innovative park designs and engaged in a wide variety of other project types —from site plans for single-family residences to master plans for new communities—commissions fueled by the dramatic increase in population and economic prosperity in the Bay Area in the postwar years. Before turning to a detailed analysis of Royston's specific parks of the period 1945–1965, it will further our understanding of these works to locate them in the Bay Area's design climate of the late 1940s and decade of the 1950s. Four aspects of this climate merit special attention: its explosive, unprecedented growth; typical projects of the landscape architectural offices in the region; prevailing concepts of park design contemporaneous with Royston's work; and ideas for planning suburbs shared by Royston and many of the park and recreation directors and planning professionals with whom he collaborated. Following this discussion, a brief analysis of Royston's own design theory and method will complete our contextual overture to the case studies.

13. SITE-PLANNING PROJECT, 1949. ROBERT ROYSTON'S URBAN DESIGN STUDIO, UNIVERSITY OF CALIFORNIA, BERKELEY. HINTS OF ROYSTON'S "LANDSCAPE MATRIX" CAN BE SEEN IN THIS STUDENT'S WORK. [EDA, UCB]

14. A STUDIO CRITIQUE, CIRCA 1949. [EDA, UCB]

15. ROYSTON AND HIS PARTNERS, 1972. FROM THE LEFT: ROYSTON, ASA HANAMOTO, LOUIS ALLEY, KAZ ABEY, PAT CARLISLE, AND HAROLD KOBAYASHI. [RHAA]

16. ROYSTON AT AGE 87 REVISITING HIS DESIGN FOR CENTRAL PARK IN SANTA CLARA. [MARC TREIB, 2005]

CHAPTER THREE

Bay Area Design, 1945–1965, and Its Precedents

When Robert Royston sailed through the Golden Gate in 1945 to resume his career as a landscape architect, the Bay Area was on the verge of the largest and most rapid expansion in its history. This explosive growth created a heady atmosphere for new practices, bringing Royston numerous commissions that tested his ideas in the arena of public work. It also challenged him to deal with the complexities of the political realm and to develop a park planning strategy for the rapidly growing suburbs, which to him often appeared to be degenerating into a nightmarish chaos lacking both order and amenity.

UNPRECEDENTED POPULATION GROWTH

California had witnessed dramatic growth in the Gold Rush of the 1840s and the prosperous years just prior to the Great Depression. However, the primarily suburban growth of the postwar years would be hard to believe if the statistics were not there to verify it. This unprecedented expansion belonged to the decade of the 1950s, often dubbed the "American Era," which encompassed the prosperous years of the presidency of Dwight D. Eisenhower. It was a time when the United States was the strongest economic and military power in the world, a time of high optimism and faith in a better future—a future that seemed assured

until its bright sky was darkened by the Cold War and its threat of thermonuclear holocaust.

In 1946 there remained a considerable amount of open land in the Bay Area—that 7,000-square-mile region comprising nine counties, sixty-six municipalities, and the cities of San Francisco and Oakland. If at that time we had chartered a low-level reconnaissance flight from San Francisco Airport, we would have immediately noticed several large areas of agricultural land between the small towns and cities on the San Francisco peninsula. Most of this land would have been planted in fruit orchards and truck gardens. If we winged a bit farther south over the northern Santa Clara Valley, the orchards and truck gardens would have been even more numerous, with a sprinkling of sleepy agricultural market towns such as Gilroy and Morgan Hill, the latter where Royston attended high school. Banking northward along the East Bay over San Leandro we would have seen open farmland, and a bit farther to the north over the expanse of Contra Costa County an extensive grid of apricot orchards and walnut groves. In a final pass over Marin County, north of San Francisco, we would have looked down on many acres of pastureland for dairy herds, and vineyards and field crops encircling small agricultural towns that had grown little for

17. LADERA COOPERATIVE HOUSING, NEAR PALO ALTO, 1945–49. THIS WAS ROYSTON'S FIRST ATTEMPT AT A LANDSCAPE MATRIX. [EDA, UCB]

18. THE STANDARD OIL ROD AND GUN CLUB, POINT RICHMOND, 1950. THE FIRST OF ROYSTON'S PARK DESIGNS TO BE BUILT. [EDA, UCB]

decades. Within ten years, much of this agricultural land on the fringes of towns and cities would be awash with detached single-family homes, garden apartments, shopping centers, new industrial plants, and freeways. The astronomical growth that transformed this mosaic of agricultural and urban land was to occur primarily on its suburban edges and not in its pre-existing urban cores, and along these edges Royston was to design most of his new parks.[27]

Although this is a well-documented narrative, a brief retelling will serve to remind us just how quick and vast the growth was. The war years were an overture, as workers poured into the area to labor in the shipyards, munitions plants, supply depots, and other war-related industries that produced and transported much of the hardware for the Pacific Theater. A dramatic example is the small city of Richmond near the Kaiser shipyards, which grew in three years from about 23,500 to 100,000 people, placing an enormous strain on its housing and infrastructure.[28] The boom further accelerated after the war, fueled by industrial expansion, the acute housing shortage, and generous support of home mortgages by the Federal Housing Authority and the so-called GI Bill. Jobs with high wages were also a potent catalyst. Furthermore, the ever-beguiling

Arcadian myth of California as a paradise blessed with a mild climate, beautiful unspoiled landscape, and abundant economic opportunity served as a powerful stimulus. This alluring myth—sustained by such diverse sources as booster rhetoric, Hollywood films, orange-crate labels, popular magazines like *Sunset*, and a host of other factors—was vigorously reasserted in the postwar period by the same agencies.[29] For thousands of servicemen who had embarked from the ports of Oakland and San Francisco for the Pacific War, it was more than fantasy although it may have been shaped by the naiveté of first impressions. In any case, they had glimpsed it firsthand, liked what they saw, and vowed to dwell there after the war. Of those fortunate enough to survive, a substantial number realized that dream.

From 1940 to 1950 the urban population of California grew by 47 percent, the greatest increase in the urban population of any state. From 1950 to 1960 it expanded by 56.4 percent and again led the nation. If we zoom in for a close-up of the Bay Area in 1940, the total population was about 1,735,000. By 1950 it had increased to nearly 2,681,000. A particular flash point was the West Bay, especially the San Francisco peninsula (excluding the city itself). This area grew by 97 percent in this decade and expanded again by an additional 80 percent from 1950 to 1960. Santa Clara County alone doubled its population to 620,000 in the six-year period from 1953 to 1959.[30] In the West Bay area these were the early days of what is now referred to as Silicon Valley, which gave birth to Hewlett-Packard, Litton Engineering, Varian Associates, and a host of other electronics industries nourished by the Cold War's military contracts and close cooperation with the research facilities at nearby Stanford University in Palo Alto. Somewhat later this boom in electronics would be augmented by the dizzying growth of the semiconductor industry with its bevy of new companies in an almost perpetual state of cloning themselves with the aid of venture capitalists. Royston designed many of his most innovative parks for the affluent, homogeneous populations of these rapidly growing West Bay municipalities, with their healthy budgets and outdated and undersized park systems.

The majority of this population growth was highly dispersed and of low density throughout most of the vast nine-county, 150-by-60-mile urban fabric of the Bay Area. The chemistry of this pattern has long been well known: the enduring preference for the single-family house; low interest rates; abundant land on urban perimeters; the mobility facilitated by the automobile; the technology of the freeway; and the truck transport able to service shopping centers, industrial plants, and office parks, thus freeing them from dependence on rail lines. Stonestown Galleria, one of the first regional shopping centers to appear, was located close to Park Merced, the venue of Royston's early design work with Thomas Church. James E. Vance Jr. has aptly described this growth pattern as the development of a "synopolis," or a "metropolis of realms." Each realm, in the case of the Bay Area, consists of the smaller municipalities such as Palo Alto and Santa Clara and the larger cities of San Francisco and Oakland, which stand in relationship to each other as "functional equals." As a whole the area operates as a group of individual parts working in concert to produce a total urban economy.[31] Peirce F. Lewis coined an appropriate term for this phenomenon, "the galactic city."[32] It is, of course, the city we have been building in the United States since Henry Ford's mass-produced Model T democratized the automobile and sped up the pace of decentralization that has characterized American urban development throughout its history. The trend is by no means confined to the Bay Area alone.

LANDSCAPE ARCHITECTURAL PRACTICE, 1945-1965

During Royston's first two decades of professional practice in San Francisco, the practice of landscape architecture in the Bay Area was among the most active and innovative in the nation. Several intellectual, economic, and social planets aligned themselves to bring this about. The postwar population growth and economic boom helped support an increasing number of professional offices. The spirit of collaboration among landscape architects, architects, planners, and engineers that flourished in the prewar years continued to foster a rich exchange of ideas and lucrative joint commissions. In 1949, Berkeley's landscape architecture program was restructured as a full-fledged department chaired by Royston's mentor, Leland Vaughan. Vaughan and his faculty revised the curriculum to emphasize the modernist approach to design pioneered before the war by Thomas Church, Dan Kiley, James Rose, and Garrett Eckbo. This new emphasis was reinforced by visiting practitioners such as Theodore Osmundson, Lawrence Halprin, Douglas Baylis, and Geraldine Knight Scott, all of whom were experimenting with new ways of using space and materials. Young, full-time faculty sympathetic to modernism—R. B. Litton Jr., Francis Violich, Mai Arbegast,

Robert Tetlow, and of course Royston himself—joined the department. The 1948 shift in the name of the department's student publication from *Axis* to *Space* heralded the new emphasis.[33] The result was a steady stream of graduates primed to experiment with new design perspectives, many of whom were hired by established firms or began their own practices in the region. As previously noted, Royston's partners Asa Hanamoto and David Mayes had been his students at Berkeley.

In the immediate postwar period, Thomas Church was the most distinguished local professional and commanded a national reputation. Several talented young designers such as Douglas Baylis and Lawrence Halprin worked in the Church office before setting out on their own. By the mid-1950s other professionals were active in the area. Besides Royston and his co-workers, they included Geraldine Knight Scott, Ned Rucker, Helen Van Pelt, John Carmack, Kathryn Stedman, Amedee Sourdry, William Penn Mott, and R. B. Litton Jr.[34] This dynamic community of professionals and academics became a crucible for design theory, and from it emerged two of the most important books on landscape architecture in the decade of the 1950s—Garrett Eckbo's *Landscape for Living* (1950) and Thomas Church's *Gardens Are for People* (1955). In particular, Royston's thirteen-year partnership and lifelong friendship with Eckbo enabled him to sharpen his own design theory through dialogue with his distinguished colleague.[35]

Until the early 1950s most Bay Area landscape architects focused their efforts on commissions for private gardens and residential site plans, a clear reflection of the exploding market in housing and California's long-standing tradition of outdoor living. Some professionals, Church, for one, chose to retain this focus while by decade's end many were expanding their practices to include larger-scale projects such as campus plans, office parks, hospital grounds, shopping centers, and public housing projects.[36] Royston's firm followed this trend.

In the first decade after the war, commissions to design parks remained scarce despite a trend toward expansion of design practices. Several factors were responsible: The lean budgets of the war years persisted in many park departments. As a result, most parks were designed by park employees with little training, who often simply refurbished older parks that were in need of immediate surgery. Funds to acquire new parkland simply were not available. This helps explain why Royston's first two park commissions were from private clients, Ladera Cooperative Housing near Palo Alto (1945–49) and the Standard Oil Rod and Gun Club at Point Richmond in the North Bay (1950) (see figures 17, 18, page 30). The situation changed as rapid suburban growth both increased the tax revenues of many municipalities and overloaded the capacity of their existing parks. The election of Democrat Edmund G. Brown to the governorship in 1958 also encouraged the expansion of park work since Brown's administration implemented moderate tax increases to provide much-needed recreation facilities, schools, and highways.[37] Thus, by the mid-1960s, park funding had improved dramatically, and Royston spent much of the remainder of his career designing public parks in the suburbs.

THEORIES OF PARK DESIGN AND SUBURBAN PLANNING, 1945-1965, AND THEIR PRECEDENTS

Few terms in the lexicon of landscape architecture have changed so often as the term "park," and few terms have fluctuated so markedly between clarity and ambiguity. This chameleon-like history is not the caprice of fashion but results from the emergence of new cultural values. In its essence landscape design is the giving of form to values: when values change, new designs appear. For the Assyrian King Assurbanipal in the seventh century B.C.E. parks were walled precincts in which to hunt lions, muster armies, celebrate military victories, and control floods. Eighteenth-century English gentry strolled and enjoyed scenery, discussed politics and philosophy, and hunted foxes in parks that were pictorially composed, didactic, allegorical landscapes.

The history of park design in the United States exhibits similar shifts of meaning from the 1860s well into the 1940s when Royston began to design parks for rapidly changing suburbs.[38] Calvert Vaux and Frederick Law Olmsted's mid-nineteenth-century definition of park resonated well into the early twentieth century. According to them, a park should address specific problems of the rapidly emerging American industrial city—its terrible slums, ethnic and racial tensions, chaotic traffic, poorly planned growth, life-threatening health hazards, disparities of wealth, and hectic, stressful routines. To deal with these issues, a park performed three primary functions: The experience of its spacious and varied landscape of open meadows and dense forests provided a valuable counterpoint to the nerve-racking hubbub of the urban environment and, in so doing, relieved stress and restored physical and psychic energy, and economic productivity. Its facilities and planned events reduced social tensions by

bringing together citizens of diverse ethnic and economic backgrounds for lighthearted recreation such as strolling, boating, and band concerts. Finally, the park's abundant vegetation functioned as the lungs of the city, filtering dangerous pollutants from the air. To achieve these ends, a park should be planted primarily in the pastoral and picturesque vocabularies developed in eighteenth- and nineteenth-century England. It should encompass hundreds of acres so that its thera-peutic power could function effectively. And because facilities for active sports would interfere with the park's restorative function, they should be situated elsewhere, in some cases adjacent to the park. For the same reason, museums, and zoos were best located in other spaces as well (figure 19).[39]

Royston accepted much of the restorative tradition of park design pioneered by Olmsted and Vaux in their work on New York's Central Park and refined and modified by other lead-ing nineteenth-century landscape architects such as Horace S. Cleveland, Ossian Simonds and later, Jens Jensen. Royston believes a lushly planted park can relieve stress and restore energy. He also affirms that one can delight in the beauty of plants simply for the sake of the pleasurable experience, which in itself is worthwhile.[40] Hence his parks include

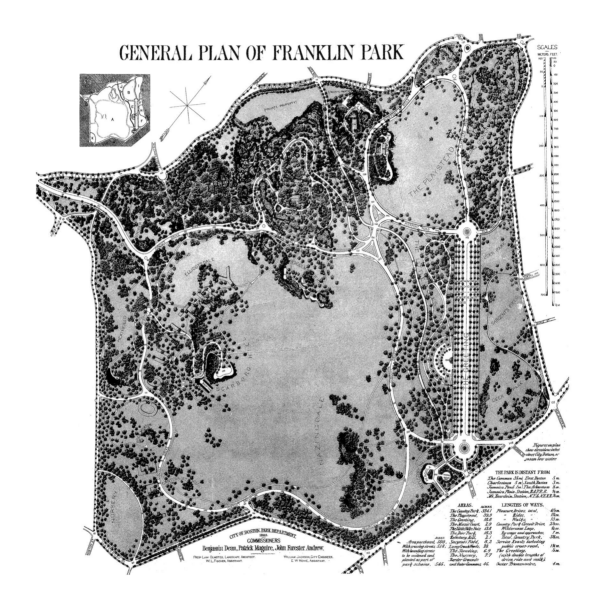

GENERAL PLAN OF FRANKLIN PARK

19. FRANKLIN PARK, BOSTON, MASSACHUSETTS, 1885. FREDERICK LAW OLMSTED. ONE OF OLMSTED'S MOST SOPHISTICATED DESIGNS, WHICH ACCOMMODATES ACTIVE RECREATION IN THE "ANTE PARK" SITUATED IN THE EASTERN PORTION OF THE SITE. [FREDERICK LAW OLMSTED HISTORIC SITE, BROOKLINE, MASSACHUSETTS (HEREAFTER FLOHS)]

groves of trees for quiet repose and contemplation as well as areas of floral display.

However, he differs from Olmsted and Vaux in a number of ways. He affirms that small parks can be just as effective therapeutically as large ones and believes they should include facilities for active sports and other amusements to allow a wide range of choices.[41] As for his design vocabulary, it derived from twentieth-century modernist architecture and painting and is far removed from that of his nineteenth-century predecessors. Also, his occasional floral displays would be anathema to Olmsted, who believed such features called too much attention to themselves and detracted from the therapeutic power of pastoral scenery.

While differing from Olmsted and Vaux and their peers on a number of key points, Royston agrees with yet another fundamental principle of their theory. Early on in their work Olmsted and Vaux conceived of a park not as an isolated entity but as part of a system of parkways and other types of recreational spaces; such a system would lend order to a city's plan, enhance the lives of its inhabitants, and perform useful work such as flood control.[42] The classic example is Olmsted's "Emerald Necklace" in Boston, which includes a large regional park, an arboretum, an artificial marsh that served to control floods, and

tree-lined parkways connecting outlying neighborhoods to the central city (figures 20, 21). This vision of parks as part of a larger system for ordering cities profoundly influenced subsequent designers. Royston's concept of suburban parks as an interconnected matrix of various park types ranging from small neighborhood parks to larger community parks is rooted in this nineteenth-century vision of comprehensive systems.

Royston's concept of types of recreation is also derived from Olmsted and Vaux. They classified various recreation activities as "exertive" (active sports and pursuits requiring focused attention such as chess) or "receptive" (enjoyment of scenery, spontaneous gatherings in large groups, picnicking, and strolling as relief from mental fatigue), and these types became an almost universal norm. In the early part of the twentieth century the terminology was changed to "active" and "passive," categories still in use today.[43] Royston, too, employs these terms.

Beginning in the late nineteenth century, urban reformers promoted new types of recreation spaces that influenced park design in ways that went beyond the theories of Olmsted and Vaux and their peers.[44] Their basic ideas were still influential in the late 1940s when Royston began his park work.

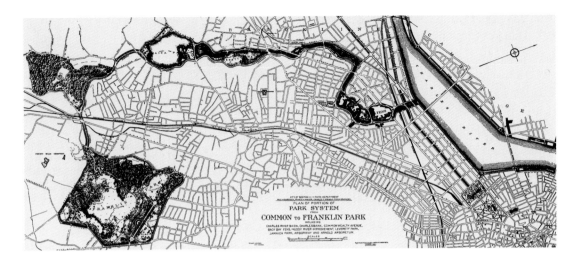

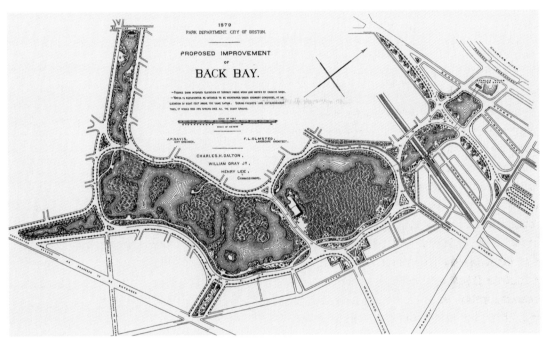

20. BOSTON PARK SYSTEM, 1894. FREDERICK LAW OLMSTED. THE ENTIRE SYSTEM IS CONNECTED BY PARKWAYS THAT JOIN WITH A MAJOR BOULEVARD LEADING TO THE CENTER OF THE CITY. [FLOHS]

21. BACK BAY FENS, BOSTON PARK SYSTEM, 1879. FREDERICK LAW OLMSTED. THIS TOTALLY ARTIFICIAL MARSH SERVED AS A RETENTION BASIN TO PREVENT FLOODS. [FLOHS]

The most important new development was the movement in Boston and Chicago in the late nineteenth and early twentieth centuries to establish small playgrounds in the poorer neighborhoods of cities to improve the safety and welfare of children. By the beginning of World War II, this movement had expanded nationwide to include recreation for adults in these areas as well. Such parks were to serve as agents of social reform that would encourage good citizenship through planned activities and wholesome outlets for physical exercise (figure 22). In some cases park designers grafted these new recreation facilities onto older, nineteenth-century parks in the Olmsted-Vaux tradition or combined them with passages of restorative scenery in new smaller-scale parks of five to forty acres to produce a hybrid serving both "passive" and "active" recreational needs (figure 23). Their programs were highly structured and supervised by specially trained adult recreation leaders. Some of these new spaces served one function only, such as playgrounds for young children or "playfields" for teenage and adult team sports.

During this period national nonprofit organizations—the National Recreation Association, the American Institute of Park Executives,

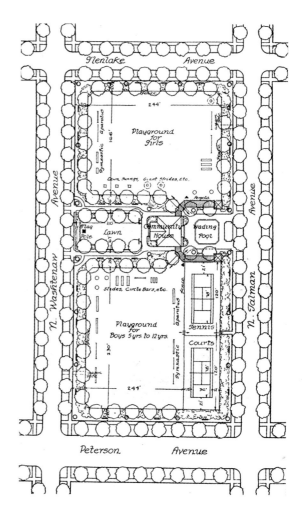

22. GREEN BRIER PARK, RIVER PARK DISTRICT, CHICAGO, ILLINOIS, 1920. JACOB L. CRANE, JR., DESIGNER. A 3.3-ACRE NEIGHBORHOOD PLAYGROUND SIMILAR IN DESIGN TO THOSE RECOMMENDED BY HENRY HUBBARD. [*PLAY AREAS, THEIR DESIGN AND EQUIPMENT*, 1928]

the Playground and Recreation Association of America—were established to promote good design. They soon began to publish precise guidelines for recreation spaces of varying scale and function using methodologies derived from the social sciences such as on-site observations, user surveys, and questionnaires targeting park administrators, leaders of supervised recreation activities, and maintenance personnel. Noting projections for a shorter workweek, earlier retirement age, and higher income resulting in increased leisure time, these guidelines placed more and more emphasis on active recreation as a wholesome pursuit that was morally beneficial.[45] This point of view continued well into the 1950s and 1960s and influenced the city councilors, park administrators, and recreation directors with whom Royston worked. His clients were especially influenced by this approach towards park design, which classified parks as functional types derived from social-scientific analysis (figure 24).

Indeed, during this period two questions had to be addressed to prevent park design from becoming a stew of rich but arbitrary ingredients. What was the function of each park type? And how were these various types to be ordered into a coherent park system to serve the public welfare?

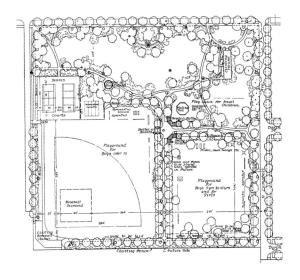

23. PAUL REVERE PARK, RIVER PARK DISTRICT, CHICAGO, ILLINOIS, 1925. A TYPICAL EXAMPLE OF A HYBRID PARK DESIGN SERVING "ACTIVE" AND "PASSIVE" RECREATIONAL ACTIVITIES. [PLAY AREAS, THEIR DESIGN AND EQUIPMENT, 1928]

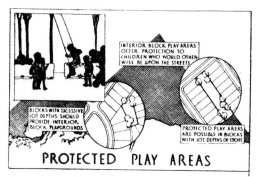

PROTECTED PLAY AREAS

SUPERVISED SCHOOL PLAYGROUNDS

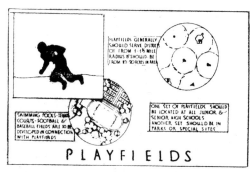

PLAYFIELDS

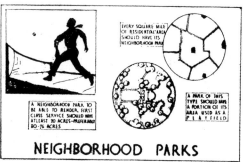

NEIGHBORHOOD PARKS

Henry V. Hubbard, professor of landscape architecture at Harvard and co-author of the widely influential text *An Introduction to the Study of Landscape Design*—first published in 1917—dealt with these questions decisively and shaped the discussion of park design for much of the twentieth century. He pioneered the development of a coherent classification of recreation spaces. First set forth in 1914 and repeated in his 1917 textbook, it was well received by park administrators and city planners, and in a modified form remains in use today in many municipalities.[46]

Hubbard's classification clearly differentiated types of park and recreation facilities based on scale and function. It insisted park systems be integrated into a total city plan. It indicated the optimum size and location for the facilities and outlined basic methodologies of the social sciences for generating precise design guidelines. Hubbard divided recreational spaces into eight types, ranging from large "reservations" on the fringes of cities, through "country parks," to smaller neighborhood "playgrounds" no more than a quarter-mile distant from their users (figure 25).[47]

Hubbard's arguments for size, distance from home, and recreational function were grounded

24. DIFFERENT TYPES OF RECREATION FACILITIES RECOMMENDED FOR A "MODERN PARK AND RECREATION SYSTEM," 1928. BARTHOLOMEW AND ASSOCIATES, ST. LOUIS, MISSOURI. [*PARKS, A MANUAL OF MUNICIPAL AND COMMUNITY PARKS*, 1928 (HEREAFTER *PARKS*)]

25. *(OPPOSITE PAGE)* DIAGRAM SHOWING WHERE CHILDREN LIVE WHO USE DES MOINES, IOWA, PLAYGROUNDS, 1925. BARTHOLOMEW AND ASSOCIATES, ST. LOUIS, MISSOURI. HENRY HUBBARD'S WORK INSPIRED SUCH STUDIES. [*PARKS*]

not in intuition but in the tenets of social science. He based his guidelines on questionnaires sent to designers, recreation supervisors, and park administrators in positions to judge the adequacy of various facilities. His collation of data yielded guidelines that approach the precision of a Swiss watch. For example, he stressed that one must know the population density of the city area served and what percentage of that population is likely to use the park at any one time. Such criteria applied to, say, a playground yielded the following recommendations apt to evoke skepticism or admiration depending on one's belief in the efficacy of social science:

Recognized one-quarter mile as an effective radius, a population of two hundred people per acre, fifty of whom were children under twelve, and one-third of whom might be expected to use the playground at the same time, the maximum size of the playground should be seven acres.[48]

Clearly, this kind of design "cookbook" could easily stifle a designer's ability to create new and engaging parks and lead to a kind of minimum standard, "one size fits all" approach that overlooks the particular needs of people in areas of ethnic and economic diversity. However, Hubbard did not intend his typology to serve as an inflexible norm that would substitute for rigorous thinking. Rather, it

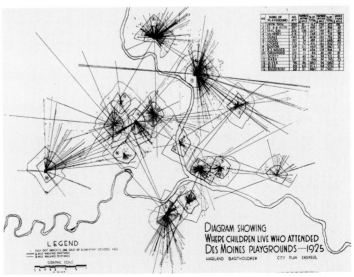

DIAGRAM SHOWING
WHERE CHILDREN LIVE WHO ATTENDED
DES MOINES PLAYGROUNDS ----- 1925
HARLAND BARTHOLOMEW   CITY PLAN ENGINEER

LEGEND

was a point of departure based on observations of informed individuals that could shape discussion and offer guidelines that could be revised by ongoing inquiry. Many park executives and city planners found it helpful, especially when tight budgets required them to rely on in-house designs by individuals with little design education.

With slight refinements and redefinitions, Hubbard's system of classification remained influential well into the post–World War II period. It was echoed in leading journals such as *Parks and Recreation* and *Recreation* that addressed park administrators and recreation supervisors. George D. Butler's widely read book *Recreation Areas, Their Design and Equipment*, first published in 1928 and updated in 1947, contains a system of classification similar to Hubbard's and very precise guidelines for the size and programs of various park types. Another important work, L. H. Weir's classic two-volume *Parks, A Manual of Municipal and County Parks* (1928), offers a similar taxonomy of parks and playgrounds.[49]

Weir's discussion of the benefits of parks encapsulates many of the principal ideas in circulation on the eve of Royston's postwar career: Parks improve one's physical health by offering opportunities for wholesome exercise. They offer outdoor experiences that relieve the stress and ill effects of a sedentary life and the repetitive work routine typical of an industrial society. They cater to humanity's need to "experience beauty," especially the "beauty of nature." They provide educational opportunities for such pursuits as nature study and offer venues for the expression of one's musical and artistic talents through neighborhood concerts and painting classes. They foster neighborhood spirit by bringing people together for shared activities and provide safety for children in play spaces removed from the dangers of the street. Their "wholesome" leisure opportunities help prevent juvenile delinquency. Finally, parks increase property values in the neighborhoods where they are located.[50]

Royston at the beginning of his park work in the late 1940s agreed with much of this theory, especially its emphasis on the positive social and psychological effects of parks and the necessity to observe firsthand how parks are used in order to create better designs.[51] His parks embody a wide range of activities similar to the ones Weir, Hubbard, and others envisioned. And, as noted, he collaborated with planners who accepted a similar taxonomy of park types and design guidelines based on a social science methodology. Here the similarity ends, since Royston's vision of parks was far more comprehensive. It was grounded in a theory of city planning that went well beyond Weir's thinking and the ideas expressed by most of the design manuals sponsored by the nonprofit recreation organizations. For Royston a system of park classification must be viewed in the wider context of a comprehensive theory of urban and suburban planning. Otherwise, such a system would be superficial and of little use.

THE PLANNING OF SUBURBS AND THE ROLE OF PARK SYSTEMS

Royston never viewed his suburban parks as isolated entities. He and several of the city planners and park department executives with whom he worked held definite views of how rapidly growing suburbs should be planned and how *park systems*, not just individual parks, were an integral part of their structure. Royston derived his ideas on the design of suburbs from his own wide reading in the literature of urban planning by such authors as Frederick Law Olmsted, Horace S. Cleveland, Lewis Mumford, Clarence Perry, and Ebenezer Howard, as well as careful study of innovative site plans such as Radburn, New Jersey, and Greenbelt, Maryland. He was also familiar with the ongoing discussion in professional journals; his office subscribed to *Parks and*

Recreation and *Recreation*. His urban design studios at the University of California, Berkeley, from 1947 to 1951 allowed him and his students to experiment with suburban planning strategies, and he brought the results to bear on his own practice. Royston was not driven by an obsession to be "original" or avant-garde. If an idea was "good," which for Royston meant that it served the welfare of those for whom he designed, he readily adopted it from others and tested it in his built work.[52]

Royston's ideas on suburban planning were nourished by many sources, but he acknowledges one publication as especially influential.[53] This was *Planning the Neighborhood*, a ninety-page document issued in 1948 by the federal government. At Berkeley he assigned it as required reading in his urban design studios and used it as the conceptual basis for projects (see figure 13). In the 1950s the planning commissions of such West Bay cities as Palo Alto and Santa Clara, where Royston did much of his park work, attempted to implement many of its recommendations.[54] The study was sponsored by a group with the rather elaborate title of the American Public Health Association Committee on the Hygiene of Housing and authored by its subcommittee on environmental standards, chaired by Frederick J. Adams. The subcommittee drew upon the expertise of city planners, landscape architects, architects, recreation directors, park executives, engineers, and government specialists in the area of housing. Brief and to the point, the booklet was accepted as normative by many city planners, park system executives, and recreation directors in California. It built upon the discussion of park types and design guidelines initiated by Henry Hubbard and refined in various articles in professional journals and books.

Planning the Neighborhood had the ring of a manifesto. It proclaimed that the acute housing shortage in the United States constituted a crisis, and it set forth the means to address this crisis in a clear and confident manner. It proposed a planning strategy that would both serve the health and safety of existing cities and their rapidly expanding suburbs and instill in their inhabitants a sense of community and civic responsibility. The key strategy was to create a well-defined group of interrelated cellular units characterized as "neighborhoods."[55]

The study defined a "neighborhood" as "the area within which residents may all share the common services, social activities and facilities required in the vicinity of the dwelling."[56] The size of a neighborhood should be determined by the "service area of an elementary school."

This will vary, but the ideal configuration is a school located no more than one-quarter mile from the children it serves. An ideal neighborhood should be no larger than 5,000 and will usually range from 2,000 to 5,000. The school, which defines the scale of the neighborhood, should serve dual roles as a place for education and as a center for meetings and social activities that will nourish a sense of community.[57]

There was nothing especially new or original about these recommendations. They had been articulated in 1929 in the work of Clarence Perry and in 1943 by N. L. Engelhardt as well as a host of other planning theorists.[58] Many of these ideas were based in part on census data, which revealed the large percentage of married couples with children in the American population. According to the official United States census of 1940, 52 percent of all households were married couples with children under twenty-one. Single adults numbered 8.6 percent, and a scant 13.5 percent were couples without children. The average family size varied mostly from three to six persons.[59]

The study stressed the importance of parks. It argued quite emphatically that a park system calibrated to the needs of a city's inhabitants is necessary for their well-being. Group recreation in parks also is a key means of "fostering good social relationships."[60] Such parks should provide "active" and "passive" recreation and serve all age groups, but special attention should be given to mothers and infants, families, and the elderly. The study argues that a park system should bring order to the city and add cohesion to its neighborhood cellular units by tying together "all parts of the neighborhood in order to create a feeling of continuous open space through the development."[61] The precise taxonomy of parks and recreation spaces, based on recommendations set forth by the National Recreation Association, which had refined Hubbard's categories through further sociological research, is brief and straightforward: neighborhood playgrounds, neighborhood parks, district parks (a district is a group of neighborhoods), citywide parks, playfields, regional parks, and special types of spaces such as urban plazas and the areas around municipal buildings. The study notes that wherever possible parks should be combined with school sites to save on land acquisition costs and avoid duplication of facilities (figure 26).[62]

This study clearly shaped the ideas of Royston and many of the public officials with whom he collaborated. They viewed parks and recreation spaces in terms of active and passive activities and categorized them according to types with different functions and scales serving a variety of age groups. They also conceived such spaces as a total system of interrelated parts that served to order the urban realm, whether it be inner city or suburban fringe—an urban realm ideally manifesting a cellular structure of discrete neighborhood units, each centered on a multi-use elementary school located in a park setting. Early in his career Royston coined the term "landscape matrix" to characterize this system of spaces.

Another publication decisively influenced ideas on park design in the mid-1950s, just when Royston was undertaking some of his most important commissions, notably Krusi and Mitchell Parks. Unlike *Planning the Neighborhood*, which addressed a national audience, this work focused specifically on the state of California. Entitled *Guide for Planning Recreation Parks in California*, it appeared in 1956. The study was funded by the state and authored by an interdisciplinary, blue-ribbon committee of architects, planners, landscape architects, recreation specialists, state and local government officials, park system managers, and representatives of nonprofit groups dedicated to developing effective policies and guidelines for recreation facilities.[63] It was frequently consulted by

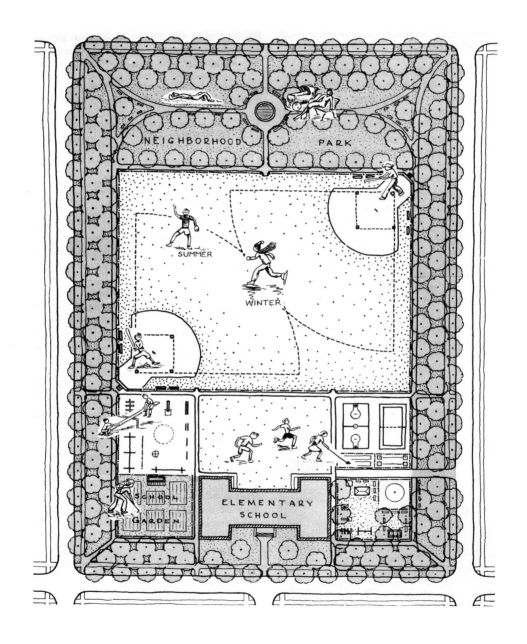

26. CONCEPTUAL PLAN FOR A NEIGHBORHOOD PARK COMBINED WITH AN ELEMENTARY SCHOOL PLAYGROUND, CLEVELAND OHIO, 1947.
[RECREATION AREAS, THEIR DESIGN AND EQUIPMENT, 1947]

many of the Bay Area municipal authorities with whom Royston worked and shaped their ideas on the location, size, and programs of parks. It had little influence on Royston's own design theory since by the time it was published he had already developed most of his basic principles. However, since he agreed with many of its recommendations, the study served as a useful reinforcement of his views and tended to foster an atmosphere of consensus between him and many of the public officials with whom he collaborated.

The study set forth "valid policies and space standards as guides for the planning of recreation parks and facilities" specifically tailored to the particular needs of the state of California. It echoed many of the basic ideas of *Planning the Neighborhood* by emphasizing the centrality of neighborhood units and the importance of park systems composed of specific types. However, it presented a much more detailed set of design guidelines for parks and was widely distributed to planning commissioners and city councils.

The *Guide* was addressed to the people of California. It opened with an affirmation of state pride but quickly moved to proclaiming a crisis in recreation facilities, which had been overwhelmed by the state's population explosion. It concluded with a plan to address this pressing issue through a comprehensive program of new park construction and encouraged designers to experiment with new types of recreation spaces. Along with its design guidelines, it included site-planning diagrams that indicated the best location for each programmatic element (playlot, playfield, etc.) in a specific type of park.[64]

The level of detail of the study's design guidelines was extraordinary, with long lists of proposed facilities and land areas calculated to one one-hundredth of an acre. However, it cautioned that these did not constitute infallible dogma but instead should be adjusted to the particular circumstances of a city or municipality.

The guidelines for the "Community Recreation Park," a type close in program and scale to many of Royston's parks, including Mitchell Park in Palo Alto and several for the city of Santa Clara, can serve as an example. A "community" park in a city of cellular neighborhoods will serve several neighborhoods.[65] It is best located no more than one-half mile from those it serves. Ideally, its land area is 20.06 acres if adjoining a high school and 32.75 acres if separate (note the calculation to two-hundredths of an acre, perhaps based in part on the high cost of land). It should contain a carefully programmed playlot for preschool children, one-quarter acre in size and featuring swings, slides, a sandbox, an open-air area for free play, "gopher holes," "climbing maze," "wheel-toy freeway," play sculpture, playhouse, "shrubs and trees," and possibly a spray pool. (As we shall see, specific details such as gopher holes, wheel-toy freeways, play sculptures, and spray pools are some of the most imaginative and engaging elements in Royston's parks. The inclusion of these elements in the *Guide* may reflect Royston's own ideas since his office had replied to a questionnaire sponsored by the study.)

In addition, this type of park would function best with a .35-acre play area for elementary school children with swings, "traveling rings," horizontal ladder, large-scale play sculpture that "children can envisage as a spaceship," lookout tower, a deep sea monster, and a "vacant lot area" in which "children can dig, carve...stage mock battles, build crude huts, and pretend they are hunting in the forest."[66] The *Guide* recommends additional elements for this multi-use park, including a field for sports (1.00 acre), a paved area for court games (1.35 acre), a "concrete slab for skating and dancing" (.15 acre), family and group picnic and barbecue areas (3.00 acres), a "park like" area for free play (2.00 acres), an "area for special events" (1.00 acre), a community center building (.75 acre), a regulation

swimming pool (.50 acre), a natural area (2.50 acres), an older peoples' center with turfed and paved areas (2.10 acres), and off-street parking (1.00 acre for 144 cars). Twenty-five percent of the site should be "landscaping" in the transitional areas and the perimeter buffer. An ideal community center building is 11,600 square feet with various rooms for arts and crafts, multipurpose rooms, kitchen, administrative offices, restrooms, teenage lounge, science study rooms, and social halls. It should also be equipped with a patio and fireplace area of 2,000 square feet. As a supplement to its long list of recommended features, the study also offers a zone diagram of a hypothetical park site indicating how to locate this complex array of functional areas in relation to one another to avoid congestion and conflicting activities (figure 27).[67]

This was the kind of hyperprecise, comprehensive, functional, typological thinking about parks grounded in social science methodology that Royston encountered in his clients: One should design parks using guidelines generated from expert opinions based on questionnaires and firsthand observations of existing recreation spaces. Such parks function best as part of a system of interrelated recreation spaces. Ideally located on school sites, they should

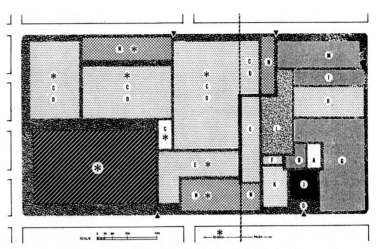

Community recreation park *adjoining* a junior high school. Diagrammatic layout showing suggested relationships among areas and facilities. Not a plan.

	Facilities	Recreation Park Adjoining Junior or Senior High School (area in acres)	Separate Recreation Park (area in acres)
A	Playlot and mothers' area	.35	.35
B	Play area for elementary school-age children	.40	.40
C	Field for sports	1.00	8.00
D	Night lighting (need for acreage depends on design)	----	.25
E	Paved area for court games	1.50	2.35
F	Concrete slab for skating and dancing	.15	.15
G	Family and group picnic and barbecue area	4.00	4.00
H	Parklike area for free play	3.00	5.00
I	Area for special events	1.00	1.00
J	Community center building	.75	1.00
K	Regulation swimming pool	1.00	2.00
L	Natural area	3.50	3.50
M	Older people's center		
	Turfed area	2.50	2.50
	Paved area	.10	.10
	Building space	.10	.10
N	Off-street parking	1.25	2.00
O	Landscaping: 35 per cent of site in transitional areas and perimeter buffer	7.21	11.45
	Total	27.81	44.15

27. ZONES-OF-USE DIAGRAM FOR A "COMMUNITY PARK." [*GUIDE FOR PLANNING RECREATION PARKS IN CALIFORNIA*, 1956]

combine active and passive recreation and be programmed to serve a full range of age groups in carefully zoned areas. It is especially important to provide special facilities for the oft-neglected elderly and teenagers. One's designs need to cater to a large range of activities: spontaneous play, team sports, science studies, and the creation of art. They should address the increasing trend toward the more "mental" recreational pursuits of a better-educated public, such as nature study or board games. Many of these activities require trained supervision. Finally, one must modify these recommendations to fit the resources of a specific municipality and fine-tune them to the needs of its particular citizens.

Royston certainly was familiar with the *Guide for Planning Recreation Parks in California*: he kept a copy of it on hand in his office. He knew these guidelines could often serve as a point of departure for discussion with citizens and municipal authorities since they had been widely distributed and accepted by many. Although he agreed with several of the recommendations, he did reject some, such as

the simplistic spatial zoning that assigned each activity to a single area and the over-quantified, pedantic scaling of various functional precincts.[68] What Royston did in his park work after the *Guide* was published in 1956 was to critique its guidelines and infuse them with his own ideas. It was to the study's credit that it encouraged designers to experiment with new concepts. Royston's parks embodied innovative spatial concepts, highly original play equipment, well-designed sports facilities, and elegant functional planting plans that transcended the zone diagrams and programmatic guidelines of the study.

The study did profoundly influence the size and the location of the parks Royston's firm was commissioned to design—matters he had no say in since these decisions were often made by public officials before he was called in. This is the reason many of his parks are almost identical in scale and location to the recommendations of the California study. In 1962 his former partner Garrett Eckbo aptly remarked: "American park design is more limited, conventional, stereotyped, repetitive, and resistant to innovation in forms than any other area of design."[69] Royston strove to break those stereotypes. He based his park designs on an ethical commitment to bring order and amenity to the rapidly expanding and often poorly planned suburbs. This ethical commitment was undergirded by a theory of design articulated by Royston as a scheme of ideas or set of principles that informed his work. Thus, if we are to understand his parks in any depth we must examine the fundamental principles of the design theory they embody.

CHAPTER FOUR

Design Theory

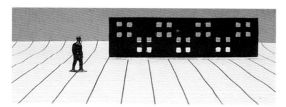

Whether Royston designed a park, an urban plaza, a residential garden, or a new town, his work was informed by a design theory consisting of a set of principles he developed early in his career. He began to develop this theory in his student days, pursued it while serving in the Navy, and refined it during the decade of the 1950s. It was a theory that in large part grew out of the challenges and complexity of his professional practice and the opportunities for experimentation in studio teaching and lecturing at the University of California, Berkeley, Stanford University, and other universities throughout the nation. Royston thrived on his design dialogues with students and colleagues. However, he was at heart a teacher-practitioner, and not a writer. He relished the creativity of professional practice and throughout most of his career preferred that his built work express his design theory. Comparing himself with his professional partner Garrett Eckbo, who was a prolific writer, Royston observed, "Garrett wrote the notes, we played the music."[70] Royston did write out the score of his "music" late in his career in a series of brief journal articles and unpublished lectures, and to understand the design principles informing his parks we need to examine those works in some detail.[71] His theoretical reflections can, for the sake of clarity, be broken down into a number of interrelated principles. However, his actual writing style tends to be more spontaneous and improvisational than systematic.

DESIGN PRINCIPLES AS "TIMELESS"

In his closely related teaching and professional work, Royston sought what he terms the "timeless principles of design," which he believes underlie the great works of landscape architecture throughout history: "In design we all search for the timeless—always a good place to begin."[72] However, he emphasized that these principles should not be codified in some kind of rigid design catechism, but rather used as a point of departure for further design investigations. They require constant testing against one's own psychological responses to various configurations of space and form as well as the responses of others. He derived these principles from a variety of sources. For example, when designing a playground, he would delve into his personal memories of play as a child, observe his own three children's play, and critique existing playgrounds. He also revisited his own designs and questioned their users about their likes and dislikes, thus establishing a clear interrelationship between his design theory and his practice.[73] In presentations to clients,

Royston often referred specifically to the "timeless" design principles embodied in his projects and illustrated them with diagrammatic sketches and models.

Royston at times speculates that these timeless principles are "genetically" or "biologically" encoded in the human psyche. In discussing the challenges of designing in a cultural context far different from one's own, he notes: "People are not that different, instinctively, biologically they are reactive in similar ways. Universal susceptibility to spatial quality exists. There is a bringing together of peoples, germinated by the biological response to place."[74] Although he does not develop these reflections at length, he does observe that other factors supplement this biological encoding. In speaking of the way in which the mind accepts or rejects design concepts and images, he reflects:

Theoretically the images of comparison are often based on the basic principles and flexibilities of space and spatial understanding tempered by our genetic heritage, what we have learned academically, and by our social and physical environment (or intuitively).[75]

In discussing this issue, Royston does not address the important question of to what extent design principles are determined by cultural values and to what extent they are primarily biological, which is, of course, a much debated issue in current design theory.

28. TYPICAL MODEL BOX STUDIES. ROYSTON USED THE MODEL BOX AS A TOOL TO TEACH HIS STUDENTS TO THINK AND DESIGN IN THREE DIMENSIONS AND TO EXPLORE THE PSYCHOLOGICAL EFFECTS OF SPACE ON INDIVIDUALS. [PPRR]

Sometimes he speaks of the biological component of our innate response to timeless design principles as a "genetic gift," which strongly implies he does not view these principles as substantially affected by cultural constructs that change over time.[76] Royston believes convincing evidence for such "timeless principles" consists to some extent in the fact that several of his parks are a half-century old and continue to delight and engage their users, who are dedicated to their preservation. The same is true of his residential gardens.

FUNDAMENTAL PRINCIPLES

Royston's brief published essays and his lecture notes as well as his own critical comments on his work articulate a basic set of oft-repeated design principles.

THE PRIMACY OF SPACE AND ITS PSYCHOLOGICAL EFFECTS

For Royston, as for many of his modernist peers, "space" is the primary medium of design. In a letter to a colleague written late in his career, he observed:

When and if I ever had time to get to a book, I would integrate the real and implied spatial intent by the abstracting [sic] the content of any space in order to test, to explain, to prove that all space has two- and three-dimensional form and space determinants that affect use, feeling and movement. That line, texture, mass, size, scale, color, smell, sound, edges, taste, etc., all play a part in spatial control and understanding of the observed and implied…This philosophy has been the foundation of all design work I have ever done.[77]

Royston stresses the importance of developing a clear and explicit understanding of space and its psychological effects, and he constantly critiqued his own work from this perspective. An examination of his teaching methods at Stanford in the mid-1950s and later in the architecture department at North Carolina State University will reveal just how central this principle was to his design theory. Royston constructed a clever device to aid his students in analyzing and critiquing the spatial configuration of their designs. This simple tool, which he dubbed "the model box," was very popular with his students. It consisted of a 48-inch-square wooden box, 18 inches high, with a translucent top to allow light to enter. Royston drilled a small viewing hole in one side and mounted the box on a revolving stand at eye level. Students placed scale models of their work in the box and then viewed their designs from the perspective of someone experiencing them on the ground. They rotated their models to explore views from different directions and cast light into the box to study shadow patterns and solar orientation. These experiments encouraged students to articulate clearly how the spaces they designed would affect their users psychologically.[78]

Often the models studied were not student designs for specific projects such as gardens or parks but were instead compositions of abstract vertical planes of varying transparency or different paving patterns that Royston had created (figure 28). Royston would gather his students around the box and manipulate the assortment of elements to expand and contract spaces, change degrees of transparency, and alter the composition of solids and voids using a variety of three-dimensional shapes. While doing so, he evoked lively discussions with such questions as, "If you increased the width of that space and reduced its degree of enclosure, how would it affect your feelings while occupying it?" or "If you layered the wall planes and increased the complexity of the paving pattern, what would be the psychological effect on the user?"

These manipulations would suggest, for instance, that a reduction of degree of enclosure and increase in scale would tend to lessen one's sense of seclusion or protection or that the use of a series of overlapping wall planes to conceal what lies beyond them piques one's curiosity. Such conclusions may appear to belabor the obvious, and in many cases they do. However, Royston believes that often designers are so obsessed with originality that they overlook the obvious to the detriment of those who use the space. Hence a thorough exploration of the psychological effects of space, regardless of how self-evident some of this may seem, is a healthy antidote to narcissism.

From Royston's belief that basic design principles are genetically encoded, it follows that he assumes one individual's psychological responses to a space would be similar to those of others. However, in real life this premise should be tested by observing how a user reacts once the space is built. The psychological responses Royston encouraged his students to elicit were positive and emotive, such feelings as serenity, curiosity, delight, adventure, mystery, and fantasy. Fear, anxiety, perplexity, and other negative states of mind were the province of other arts.

Royston supplemented these discussions with slide lectures illustrating the psychology of space with photographs of historical and contemporary sites, such as the Piazza San Marco and Rockefeller Center. In addition he discussed the issues raised by his own design work, providing students with an engaging synergy of teaching and practice. Above all,

Royston instilled in his students the fundamental notion that an art-for-art's-sake approach to design is a serious error that will in all likelihood produce projects that could be detrimental to their users and perhaps the natural environment as well. Design must always relate to human use and the positive psychological effects of space on its occupants. Like a leitmotiv in a Wagner opera, he proclaims this time and again in his late essays.[79] As we shall see, Royston's parks are prime examples of this concept of space. When reflecting on these exercises fifty years later, Royston maintains that the learning that resulted from this kind of comparative analysis was invaluable, and he can think of no better way to have communicated with his students.

THE SHARED PRINCIPLES OF THE ARTS

Royston also believes there is a strong link between the design principles of landscape architecture and the arts of dance, painting, drama, and sculpture:

Just like in dance…painting or whatever, you begin to see things in terms of structural dimension and movement. That's what good paintings are, what good landscape architecture is. These qualities exist all around us …it's all there in terms of line, form, structure, texture, sound, whatever, your eye will follow it.[80]

Furthermore, familiarity with this common ground will nurture the development of a landscape architect's design principles.

Principles of abstract painting in particular influenced Royston's landscape design, dating back to his student days at the University of California. Indeed, during his entire career, Royston has continued to explore design form through his own abstract paintings (figure 29). His understanding of the relationship of his work in garden or park design to painting is very similar to the position of Stephen C. Pepper, Professor of Philosophy and Aesthetics at the University of California, Berkeley, expressed in *Landscape Design*, the 1948 catalog of the second exhibition of works of landscape architecture sponsored by the San Francisco Museum of Art.

The creation of a garden…becomes something halfway between the making of a painting and the making of a house. It is as if the landscape architect were composing an abstract painting for people to live within. And because people are to live inside it…the functions it is to serve as a place to dig, to dine, to play games in, or read in, or nap in become also elements of its composition (figure 30).[81]

Sculpture and theater design were also important sources for Royston's concept of space: "as with a sculptor, the three-dimensional whole work is our normal task. Landscape

29. A PAINTING BY ROBERT ROYSTON, EXECUTED IN THE EARLY 1950s (DETAIL). [REUBEN RAINEY, 2003]

30. ARIAN GARDEN, MILL VALLEY, EARLY 1950s. ROYSTON'S RESIDENTIAL GARDEN PLANS OFTEN RESEMBLED LARGE-SCALE, THREE-DIMENSIONAL ABSTRACT PAINTINGS. [RHAA]

architecture also, as theatre, is not to be avoided. What we plan and build is often a stage for life and people in movement and their interaction may be the very essence of the urban landscape."[82]

This notion of the urban landscape as "a stage for life" may reflect Royston's background in theater. Indeed, his early experience as an actor may even have influenced his invention of the "model box," which resembles a model stage set with movable parts. It may also explain why he often included stages or amphitheaters in his park designs.

Also, specific currents in twentieth-century painting such as cubism and biomorphism influenced Royston's ideas of space as a design medium and suggested the forms to define it. He singles out Paul Klee, Wassily Kandinsky, Piet Mondrian, and Pablo Picasso as significant influences.[83] Marc Treib has shown how Garrett Eckbo, Royston's former partner, was especially influenced by the work of Wassily Kandinsky, with its sweeping arcs played off against rectangular forms and bold diagonal lines. Some of Royston's park work and residential site plans manifest similar forms, perhaps the result of the exchange of ideas between the partners, although they mostly worked independently of one another in the San Francisco and Los Angeles offices

(figures 31, 32). Treib has coined the apt term "biocubic" for Eckbo's work, a blend of the smooth-flowing irregular curves of biomorphism and the more angular geometries of analytical cubism.[84] The term could apply to Royston's work as well. There is indeed something of a family resemblance between Royston's and Eckbo's design vocabularies, but more like that of two first cousins. Royston's work often seems more serene and less spatially charged. It emphasizes the sweep of elegant lines with less tension created by bold, dissonant diagonals—more Mondrian and Klee and less Kandinsky—paired with a layering of analytical cubist planes (figures 33, 34). His designs for the playgrounds at Krusi, Mitchell, and Pixie parks are typical examples of this vocabulary (figure 35).

Royston believes a key reason to study painting is to observe how "movement" is embodied in composition. His plans for gardens and parks invite the eye to move from one form to another just as the experience of his built work invites exploration and movement through the designs (figure 36). He also acknowledges the strong influence of architects Mies van der Rohe and Le Corbusier on his design vocabulary, especially the spatial layering expressed in Mies's Barcelona Pavilion and other residential commissions.[85] Furthermore, his design details share some

of the elegant restraint of his former employer, Thomas Church, but without Church's more literal classicism and eclectic tendencies. The graceful curves of Royston's wooden windbreaks at the Standard Oil Rod and Gun Club and his spare angular pergolas at Mitchell Park are reminiscent of the acute sense of line in Church's gardens.

THE IMPORTANCE OF INTUITION

Royston emphasizes the centrality of intuition as a design principle, but he is not certain how to define it: "Intuition may be the subconscious speed-up of knowledge. It may be what happens in conceptual drawings as the mind accepts and rejects images (faster than any computer could ever do) which is comparative analysis."[86] At times he suggests that intuition is in part a spontaneous expression of our genetic capacity to recognize and create timeless design principles that respond to basic human needs.[87] He also affirms the primacy of intuition over a pattern-book approach to design, which, as we have seen, he rejected: "Standards in design are an effort to design with words, often to the detriment of creativity."[88] Royston distinguishes between design "standards," which are rigid and inflexible, and "principles," which, while "timeless," are open

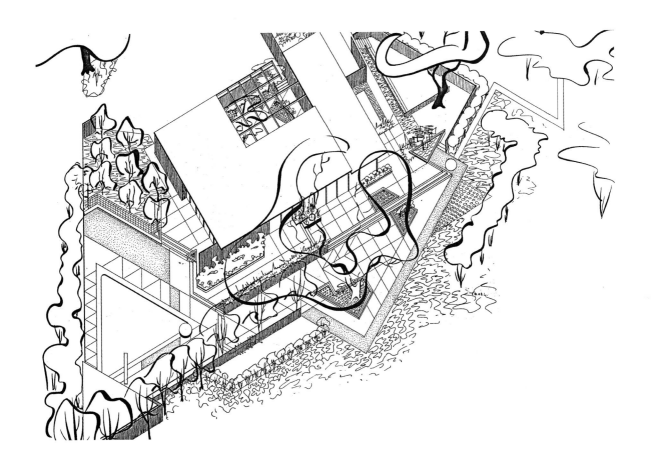

31. *(OPPOSITE PAGE)* *IN THE BLACK SQUARE*, WASSILY KANDINSKY, 1923. DEVELOPMENTS IN MODERN ART, ESPECIALLY PAINTINGS, WERE A SIGNIFICANT INFLUENCE ON ROYSTON'S DESIGN VOCABULARY. [SOLOMON R. GUGGENHEIM MUSEUM, NEW YORK]

32. APPERT GARDEN #2. MARIN COUNTY. AXONOMETRIC DRAWING. THE LAYERED PLANES AND SHARP ANGULARITY SUGGEST KANDINSKY'S INFLUENCE.. [EDA, UCB]

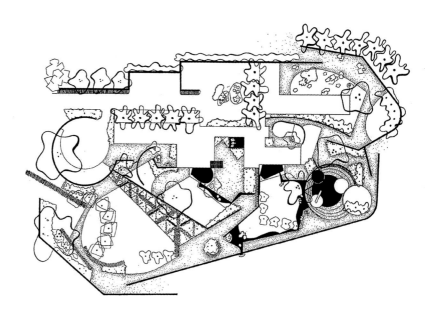

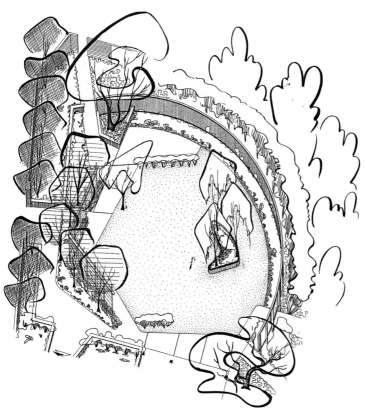

33. BURDEN GARDEN, WESTCHESTER COUNTY, NEW YORK, 1947, PLAN. GARRETT ECKBO. TYPICALLY, ECKBO'S GARDEN DESIGNS WERE MORE COMPLEX IN PLAN AND INCLUDED GREATER DYNAMIC CONTRASTS. [EDA,UCB]

34. NAIFY GARDEN, ATHERTON, 1954. ISOMETRIC SKETCH. WHEN COMPARED TO ECKBO'S MORE EXUBERANT DESIGNS, ROYSTON'S GARDEN DESIGN VOCABULARY APPEARS ALMOST SERENE. [EDA,UCB]

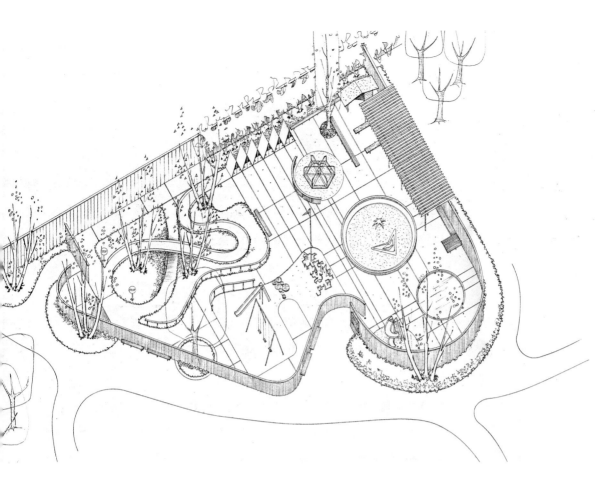

35. KRUSI PARK, ALAMEDA, 1954. ROYSTON OFTEN EMPLOYED AXONOMETRIC PLANS TO CLEARLY ILLUSTRATE THE SPATIAL VOLUMES OF HIS DESIGNS. [EDA,UCB]

36. STANDARD OIL ROD AND GUN CLUB, POINT RICHMOND, 1950. THE REDWOOD WINDBREAKS CREATE A SENSE OF FREE-FLOWING SPACE INVITING FURTHER EXPLORATION. THEY ALSO SERVE AS SUN TRAPS. [RHAA]

to discovery and modification through testing by experience.[89] (Perhaps this distinction reveals a trace element of Royston's years of frustration in dealing with the rigid standards of park design advocated by some park departments and planning officials.)

THE MULTISENSUAL NATURE OF LANDSCAPE ARCHITECTURE

Royston affirms that works of landscape architecture should engage all the senses, but acknowledges the dominance of sight in the user's experience:

Environmental quality has to do with surface, line, form, scale, volume, movement, size, social content, social function, mystery, memory, spatial implications, texture, color, sound, smell, and taste. Most of the above are related to the visual—what the eye sees is most important, but human response is the result of cumulative environmental impact.[90]

Royston often divides his parks into distinct visual units, which helps to define various functional areas. A children's playground area can be taken in at a single glance and is a striking visual composition. The same is true of more passive areas, such as serene groves of mature trees (figure 37). Scented plants and tactile surfaces such as stone, wood, and concrete also contribute to the multisensual dimension of his parks.

THE REJECTION OF STYLES AND ICONOGRAPHY

As noted, Royston emphasizes that the visual dynamics of abstract form and space evoke experiences that are engaging and pleasurable. His formal and spatial configurations do not recall or represent something else, i.e., they carry no symbolic meaning. This point of view underlies his rejection of styles: he avoids iconography and use of forms that evoke historical memories wherever possible, an approach that echoes Le Corbusier's proclamation of "the styles" as a "lie." For Royston, "style" is a preconceived design vocabulary that copies historical periods or mimics present-day work in a bow to the latest design fashion. Thus, style trumps the needs of users and bypasses rigorous investigation of design issues:

The search for movement and feeling in space and in determining form knows no boundaries, no isms such as modernism, post-modernism, historical conformity. It accepts all, the then and the now, and has much in common with great architecture, painting, sculpture, and structural engineering as well as civil, when seen or understood in the abstract…all work spatially, and sometimes with the same ingredients.[91]

37. MITCHELL PARK, PALO ALTO, 1956. NORTHWEST PICNIC GROVE. [REUBEN RAINEY, 2005]

However Royston did make exceptions to his avoidance of iconography and historical associations. If an individual client or a group of citizens wanted to include or preserve such elements, he would honor their requests. Examples are a symbolic redwood tree in Mitchell Park and the statue of Saint Clare in the Santa Clara Civic Center Park. Yet, what is most important for Royston is the immediate sensate experience of spaces and their materials, which can evoke such experiences as a feeling of mystery, comforting enclosure, or other psychological states devoid of cognitive meaning or association. Royston's position is similar to that of the eighteenth-century landscape gardener Lancelot ("Capability") Brown, who de-emphasized the popular allegorical temples and other garden elements of his day and instead stressed the intrinsic beauty of line and of the materials of the site itself, which produced a feeling of pleasure. As historian John Dixon Hunt has pointed out, Thomas Whateley, the eighteenth-century English writer on landscape gardening, characterized this approach as a shift from the "emblematic" to the "expressive."[92]

AN EMPHASIS ON TEMPORALITY

Royston also stresses the temporality of works of landscape architecture. This consists of three aspects: processional space, the organic growth of plants, and the marking of seasonal change.

His parks are designed to be experienced over time, through exploring their linked spaces or revisiting them at various seasons. In this respect they resemble music and dance, which likewise unfold over time. A typical Royston park such as Palo Alto's Mitchell Park or Santa Clara's Central Park contains circuit walks affording visitors a variety of spatial experiences and sequential views. Heavily canopied spaces deep in shadow give way to broad sunlit meadows, and a glistening fountain may appear suddenly around a bend in a path (figure 38). These walks are far more than functional connectors of various recreational zones; they provide a sense of discovery and delight. Often he plants groves of tall trees, usually redwoods, along his circuit walks to orient the stroller with point-to-point landmarks that invite further exploration (figure 39). Along the perimeters of the parks he uses large openings to the street to let passersby look deep into their interiors and observe the many activities in progress and perhaps be drawn inside (figure 40). This treatment of the edges contrasts with Olmsted and Vaux's tendency to buffer the perimeters of their parks with thick tree and understory plantings, creating a strong visual barrier between the parks and their surroundings that hermetically seals them off from the urban environment.

Royston's work also recognizes the temporality of plants, the primary materials he employs in his parks to define space. In reflecting on his development as a designer, Royston recalls:

Plant materials as individual plants never really interested me that much...Invariably I would look at them as sculpture...I saw them as building space...When you get into plant materials they are the walls. I realized they are growing walls. We did lots of experiments analyzing what the space would be as the plants matured at 5, 10, 20 years. As your material grows it is kind of wonderful to contemplate.[93]

Royston welcomed the challenge of a medium constantly changing over time. Many of his park sites were originally bare fields, devoid of trees and understory shrubs. In the initial years of occupancy, immature trees and shrubs could hardly define space effectively. To meet this challenge he employed architectural features such as curving walls, pavilions, and pergolas to provide instant spatial definition for different zones of use (figure 41). He reinforced these architectural elements, which were similar in scale and form to elements in his residential

gardens, with heavy plantings of vines, shrubs, and trees that matured over time, providing a more nuanced and powerful spatial definition of these areas (figure 42).

The third aspect of temporality for Royston is the marking of seasonal change. He believes parks should provide their users with close contact with the beauty and restorative power of natural processes.[94] Thus he uses plants to celebrate the cycle of the seasons. This aspect of his approach to planting design is especially sophisticated when compared to typical planting plans of many urban parks, consisting of lawn and a few species of trees scattered about. While often constrained by park departments' meager budgets, he nonetheless developed a diverse palette of low-maintenance trees and shrubs that display spring bloom and fall foliage as well as visually interesting winter textures and branching patterns. When deciduous shrubs and trees are used to articulate space in a Royston park, their summer and winter variations frequently provide contrasting degrees of transparency to the walls and ceilings of the park rooms they define. Fine examples of these design strategies can be found in the mature plantings of any of Royston's parks, but an especially notable instance can be seen at Mitchell Park in Palo Alto, where a wall of magnifi-

38. CENTRAL PARK, SANTA CLARA, 1960–1975. VISIBLE THROUGH THE TREES IS THE LARGE, TENT-LIKE PICNIC PAVILION. [REUBEN RAINEY, 2004]

39. CENTRAL PARK. THE REDWOOD GROVE. [REUBEN RAINEY, 2005]

40. MITCHELL PARK, PALO ALTO, 1956. ROYSTON'S PRESENTATION MODEL SHOWING OPENINGS IN THE VEGETATION ALONG THE PARK'S EDGES. [RHAA]

41. BOWDEN PARK, PALO ALTO, 1960. LOG PAVILION FRAMING A VIEW OF THE CENTRAL LAWN. [REUBEN RAINEY, 2004]

cently gnarled Hollywood junipers (*Juniperus tortulosa*) (figure 43) creates an entry to an allée of mimosa trees (*Albizia julibrissin*) (figure 44). In this instance the light structure and fine texture of the deciduous mimosa trees contrast effectively with the dark, swirling, evergreen junipers at the entrance and the massive walls of California redwoods (*Sequoia sempervirens*) that define nearby edges of the park. This tension is heightened in the spring when the new fern-like chartreuse foliage of mimosa trees is nearly obscured by clouds of fluffy pink blossoms and again in winter when their slender horizontal branches stand out against the dark green backdrop of juniper and redwood. This is but one example of Royston's overall planting design for that park that underscores the passing of time and season.

HUMAN USE DETERMINES DESIGN FORM

On first glance a park plan by Royston often reveals a formal vocabulary reminiscent of a painting by Piet Mondrian, Jean Arp, or Paul Klee, or, even more likely, one by Royston himself. A closer reading reveals his meticulous tailoring of design form to human use, a deft alchemy that transforms painterly abstractions to serve concrete human activities. Far from

being exercises in self-referential formal manipulations, the elements of his parks manifest a meticulous and sensitive accommodation of such pursuits as team sports, spontaneous play, social gatherings, civic rituals, and quiet contemplation. A Mondrian-like grid plan creates intimate enclosed spaces for private conversations. The various arms of an amoeba-like lake define zones for different activities, such as fishing, flycasting competitions, and model boat sailing. Here, the top rail of a playground fence is just high enough to form a comfortable resting place for the elbows of a standing parent. There, a concrete play structure has handholds molded to the size of a young child's hands and is just high enough to evoke a sense of risk without the possibility of serious injury. Often these features, which can be quite subtle, become more apparent as one observes the behavior of people in Royston's parks. Subordination of form to use constitutes one of the most humane and appealing dimensions of his work. His brief essays allude to it time and time again.

THE COLLABORATIVE NATURE OF DESIGN WORK

Finally Royston rejects the clichéd romantic image of the heroic designer toiling alone to produce works of consummate brilliance,

often misunderstood and rejected by the ignorant bourgeois multitude; rather he affirms, "Citizen participation in the design process is essential."[95] Furthermore, most design projects are best realized by teams representing a variety of disciplines: "The magnitude and complexity of landscape design and development demand the services of coordinated professional teams. No single individual can measure up to the strength of several who work together in an environment where mutual respect and professional competence exist."[96] Royston designed the vast majority of his suburban parks as a team effort with architects, engineers, and sculptors. His embrace of citizen participation reveals his faith in the potential of laypersons to contribute important ideas. However, he does not believe in design by majority ballot. The designer must evaluate all citizen input and bears the ultimate authority to accept or reject it. The professional responsibility of the landscape architect involves the creation of innovative designs that can transcend the suggestions of even the most gifted layperson.[97]

For over half a century Royston applied his design theory to his practice and teaching of landscape architecture, a profession he calls "preventive medicine": "We work in the realm of health, our profession can restore a marsh, purify the air, abate noise, provide systems in the city where trees will grow and people can gather, exercise and laugh."[98] On another occasion, with typical succinctness, he observes that landscape architecture "practices the fine art of relating the structure of culture to the nature of landscape, to the end that people can use it, enjoy it, and preserve it."[99]

How did Royston perform this dual role of "artist" and "physician" dedicated to the welfare of human beings and the natural environment and apply his multifaceted design principles to the creation of parks? An examination of his concept of a park as well as his manner of designing and dealing with clients will reveal how he set about the task.

42. MITCHELL PARK, PALO ALTO, 1956. PERGOLA WITH WISTERIA VINE FORMING AN ENTRY TO THE PARK FROM THE PARKING LOT. [REUBEN RAINEY, 2002]

43. MITCHELL PARK. MATURE HOLLYWOOD JUNIPERS CREATE SCULPTURAL INTEREST AND SPATIAL DEFINITION ALONG THE PARK'S EDGE. [REUBEN RAINEY, 2006]

44. MITCHELL PARK. MIMOSA ALLÉE FORMING A MAJOR PART OF THE NORTH-SOUTH AXIS. [REUBEN RAINEY, 2005]

CHAPTER FIVE

The Park and Its Design Methodology

THE "PUBLIC GARDEN"

Robert Royston, as we have noted, conceived of his parks as public gardens. Yet the term "garden" lends itself to as many definitions as the word "park." It can refer to the vegetable plots of ancient Neolithic villages and to meditation spaces almost devoid of vegetation in Zen Buddhist monasteries. A typical dictionary definition is narrow: "A plot of land used for the cultivation of flowers, vegetables, or fruit."[100] Speaking of his parks as public gardens, Royston does not mean they are spaces in which citizens may cultivate vegetables and flowers along the lines of the "community gardens" found today in many American cities. Neither is he referring to public gardens designed almost solely for the display and enjoyment of flowers, similar to the Oakland Municipal Rose Garden of 1934 or the Berkeley Municipal Rose Garden of 1940, two New Deal projects (figure 45).[101]

Royston's understanding of a garden is broader, more attuned to the types of private residential gardens he designed early on in his professional career (figure 46). These gardens address many functions. They are gathering places for family and friends. They provide play areas for children, spaces to engage in lawn games, and patios with cooking areas. They are spaces for celebrating the bonds of friendship and

45. BERKELEY MUNICIPAL ROSE GARDEN, 1940. [BERKELEY ARCHITECTURAL HERITAGE ASSOCIATION]

family and enjoying lighthearted recreation. Royston's parks are to a great extent conceived as private residential gardens writ large. Instead of catering to the recreational needs of a single family, they provide for a neighborhood or cluster of neighborhoods, depending on their scale and program. They are filled with facilities for groups of families and community organizations, such as picnic areas and elaborate playgrounds for children of varying ages. They provide community centers where interest groups, including birdwatchers, Tai Chi classes, and chess clubs, can meet. They are places to gather for civic rituals, like Fourth-of-July celebrations, or political events such as discussions of proposed zoning changes. Their extensive facilities for sports cater to individuals and organized teams. Just as the use of a private residential garden may strengthen ties between friends and family, Royston's public gardens operate in a similar fashion on a community-wide scale. Here people of all ages can congregate, play, relax, or celebrate, experiencing a sense of community identity in the midst of a culture of ever-increasing mobility, which tends to isolate individuals from one another.

Even the details of Royston's parks—vine-covered pergolas, tent-like pavilions, patio-like cooking areas, elegant wooden fences—

46. LEETE GARDEN, MARIN COUNTY, 1948. ROYSTON'S EARLY RESIDENTIAL GARDEN DESIGNS EMPHASIZED MULTI-FUNCTIONAL SPACES. IN THIS INSTANCE SCREEN FENCING AND LOW WALL DISGUISE A STEEP HILLSIDE. [RHAA]

recall smaller private gardens (figures 47, 48).[102] The design vocabulary itself is similar: overlapping walls of vegetation that create a sense of movement, dynamic "biocubic" forms, a seasonal plant palette, and elegant, understated details that express the inherent qualities of their materials. Such characteristics infuse these parks with a sense of intimacy and familiarity. This approach stands in stark contrast to several of the urban parks of the 1930s modeled on the lavish private villas of the Italian Renaissance. Typical examples are Lakecliff Park in Dallas, Trinity Park in Fort Worth, and Lindavista Park in Oakland.[103] One of the most elaborate examples is Washington, D.C.'s Meridian Hill Park, a slightly revised version of Cardinal Farnese's sixteenth-century *villino* at Caprarola transported to the Federal City a few miles from the White House.[104] Royston's parks, in contrast, recall your neighbor's garden (if she can afford a single family home) rather than the glory of the Medici or a 1920s millionaire's idea of the good life.

In accord with *Planning the Neighborhood* and *Guide for Planning Recreation Parks* in California, Royston envisioned these parks at a variety of scales and functional types, ranging from small neighborhood playlots to large city parks of fifty acres or more. However,

in none of his commissions could Royston completely achieve his goal of a "landscape matrix." But he laid the foundations for several interconnected systems in his individual park commissions, especially in Palo Alto and Santa Clara.

In addition to envisioning his parks as public gardens, Royston also claimed they were "a new art form."[105] What precisely was new about them? When compared to previous Bay Area parks their inventiveness consists in their comprehensive program of activities, their fresh design vocabulary, and their innovative children's playgrounds. This is readily apparent if one examines a typical plan for a Bay Area park that predates Royston's work, Rinconada Park in Palo Alto (figure 49).[106] This park is what Royston would call an outdoor gymnasium layered onto a scaled-down version of an Olmsted and Vaux pastoral landscape of lawn and trees. Its play zones are attached to its curvilinear walk like beads on a necklace. The walk is a connector of play areas, not an interesting promenade. Except for its bowling green, tennis courts, and theater at the west end, the park is programmed almost exclusively for the active recreation of children who attend the adjacent school. This combination of a nineteenth-century planting design and lack of programmatic

47. MARIN ART AND GARDEN SHOW EXHIBIT, 1960. THE OVERSIZED GARDEN UMBRELLA WAS A FAVORITE ELEMENT UTILIZED BY ROYSTON IN MANY OF HIS RESIDENTIAL DESIGNS. [RHAA]

48. CENTRAL PARK, SANTA CLARA, 1960-75. THE UMBRELLA-LIKE PICNIC PAVILION. [RHAA]

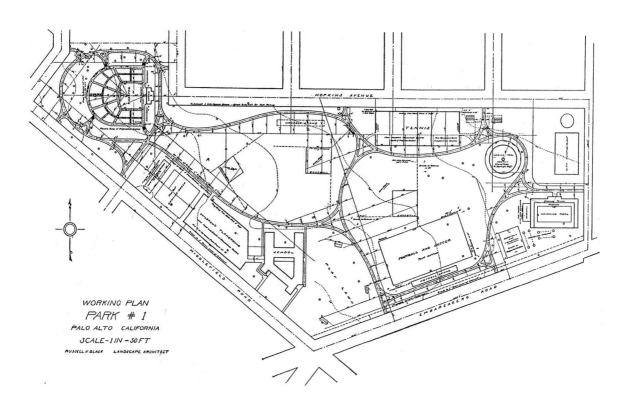

WORKING PLAN
PARK # 1
PALO ALTO   CALIFORNIA
SCALE - 1 IN - 50 FT
RUSSELL V. BLACK   LANDSCAPE ARCHITECT

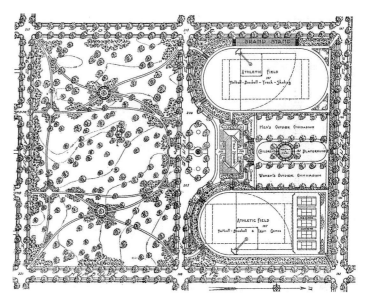

elements that cater to young and old alike contrasts sharply with Royston's parks, with their multiple facilities for a wide diversity of age groups, and fresh vocabulary of overlapping spaces and biocubic forms. While both Royston's parks and Rinconada Park contain children's playgrounds, Royston's are far more appealing, featuring pedal-car freeways, adventuresome climbing apparatuses, crawl spaces, and roller-skating areas in colorful, sculptural forms. Rinconada's prosaic galvanized steel swing sets, seesaws, and sandboxes pale in comparison.

Royston's innovations contrast with the park designs typical of other parts of the country as well. This is apparent in the 1918 plan for Folwell Park in Minneapolis, a plan characteristic of those found in journals and books prior to World War II and considered to be excellent design (figure 50).[107] A major through street clearly divides the twenty-seven-acre park into two equal zones, one for passive and one for active recreation. The passive zone is designed in the nineteenth-century mode of lawn with irregularly placed trees. Its curvilinear walk system is bilaterally symmetrical. The zone for active recreation to the north includes a fieldhouse, athletic fields, tennis courts, separate men's and women's outdoor gymnasia, and a children's playground. All of these elements are likewise ordered sym-

metrically in a typical Beaux-Arts design. While this park caters to a wider range of age groups than Rinconada Park, its spatial organization is rigid and dull, lacking the wide variety of programmatic elements and innovative play equipment typical of Royston's parks of the same scale.

About the same time Royston pioneered his new park designs, European designers such as Aldo van Eyck in Holland and Alfred Trachsel in Switzerland experimented with similar vocabularies—primarily for urban playgrounds. A decade later American landscape architects M. Paul Friedberg, Richard Dattner, and the Canadian Cornelia Hahn Oberlander proposed additional models for playgrounds. However, given their suburban rather than urban locations, Royston's parks tended to be much larger in scale with a greater variety of facilities and more effective use of plant material.

A METHOD FOR DESIGNING PARKS

By the late 1950s Royston had refined his methodology for designing parks as a "new art form" as well as his mode of presentation to government officials and the public. Royston rarely had the opportunity to choose his park sites. They were assigned to him by city planners or directors of parks and

49. RINCONADA PARK, PALO ALTO, 1925. "WORKING PLAN." A TYPICAL EXAMPLE OF A PARK ORGANIZED AS AN OUTDOOR GYMNASIUM. [PLAY AREAS]

50. FOLWELL PARK, MINNEAPOLIS, MINNESOTA, 1918. IMPROVEMENT PLAN. A TYPICAL COMBINATION OF FORMAL AND INFORMAL SPATIAL ORGANIZATION DERIVED FROM ITALIAN RENAISSANCE AND 18TH-CENTURY ENGLISH DESIGN TRADITIONS. THE ACTIVE RECREATION AREA IS ASSIGNED TO THE NORTH SECTION OF THE PARK. [PLAY AREAS]

recreation departments, and they were usually located adjacent to public schools to reduce land acquisition costs.[108] Public officials approached his firm directly and sought its services; normally he did not compete with other offices for commissions. Design programs were developed in dialogue with parks department staff and city planners. At times he presented his designs to city council meetings attended by groups of citizens, as he did in Palo Alto. At other times the parks department's director presented the designs, as was the case with Santa Clara. These design reviews resulted in few changes to the initial designs, which were usually approved without extensive discussion. During the construction process Royston worked closely with parks department officials to make whatever modifications might be necessary. Many of the parks were funded by bond issues and some were constructed in phases. Royston respected the guidelines of a municipality's comprehensive plan, but he recalls he sought to "stretch" them in "creative ways," especially if there was any potential to work toward a landscape matrix.[109]

Once given a site, Royston inspected the land firsthand and acquainted himself with the topography, drainage, soil, vegetation, microclimate, views, historical features, existing structures, immediate off-site context, and relationship to existing parks. With the agreed-upon program in mind—which he regarded as a point of departure open to revisions—the design work began. Royston alone designed most of the parks of the late 1940s to the early 1960s while his partners and office staff handled residential gardens, office parks, and other projects. From the early 1960s on, however, Royston worked as a member of an office team, having become a firm believer in the virtue of pooled wisdom. He often produced schematic drawings, turned them over to colleagues for development and completion, then "reviewed and approved every line" on the final drawings.[110]

Design usually began with a scaled topographic plan of the site. Using an overlay of tracing paper, Royston would establish a strong armature of circulation, usually a single axis or two crossing axes or a circuit walk around the site. He would then add a series of activity areas, such as tot lots, playgrounds, senior citizen facilities, and picnic table clusters, and represent them as zone diagrams precisely scaled to the dimensions appropriate to their function (figure 51). He was careful to relate these areas to his circulation armature, making certain they were located in the proper relationship to one another to facilitate their use and avoid conflict. For example, a tot lot was

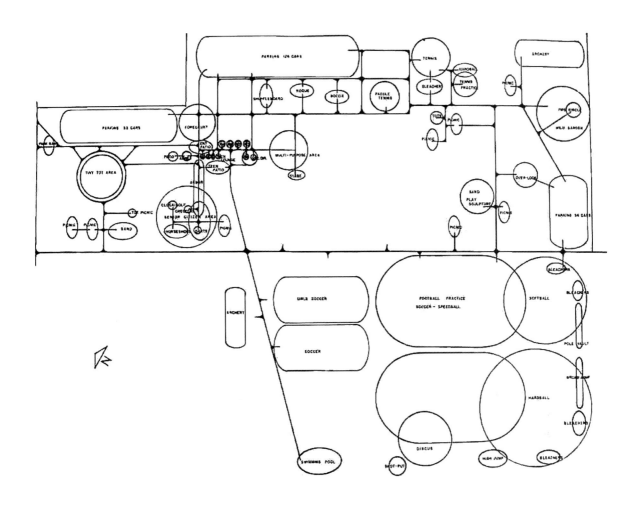

51. MITCHELL PARK, PALO ALTO, 1957. CIRCULATION AND RECREATION ZONE DIAGRAM. [EDA,UCB]

near a play area for older children so a parent or guardian with children of different ages could supervise the play of both age groups (figures 52, 53). Or sports fields for teens or adults were far removed from play areas for small children.

Once Royston was satisfied with the scaled activity diagrams, which often resembled the wiring plans of an electrical appliance, he transformed them into a more developed design. Perhaps the children's play area would be shaped into a series of three-dimensional interlocking forms for climbing, swinging, or water play. Since space was his primary medium, he visualized the park in terms of walls, floors, and ceilings in the same manner he approached his residential garden designs. He followed this approach for parks of varying scales, with the exception of small playgrounds, which were less demanding.[111]

For the most part, the park work of his contemporaries was not a source for ideas. Instead he frequently visited San Francisco's much older Golden Gate Park, observing intently how people used its wide variety of spaces.[112] And as noted, he consulted his own earlier designs for concepts judged successful by himself, park users, and park officials.

He took great care to use graphics that communicated clearly with his clients. A typical presentation combined plans with perspective sketches and models, especially emphasizing models since he knew they are more easily understood by laypersons. Some of the models used conventional materials such as cardboard, wood, and dried plants; others were constructed of one-eighth-inch layers of plate glass that were inked in plan view and stacked vertically to create striking three-dimensional depictions. These, he recalls, were especially effective although their weight and fragility were inconvenient.[113] Royston's experience as an actor, combined with his clear, unpretentious language and three-dimensional models, made him a persuasive and effective communicator. In a typical presentation he concentrated on the park design under discussion and did not show his earlier work. To reinforce his presentation he would often use slides illustrating the abstract design principles derived from the model box he had developed for teaching.[114]

52. KRUSI PARK, ALAMEDA, 1954. FOR EASIER SUPERVISION, THE TOT PLAY AREA IN THIS PARK WAS LOCATED ADJACENT TO THE PLAYFIELDS FOR OLDER CHILDREN. [RHAA]

53. KRUSI PARK. THE PLAY SCULPTURES WERE AN ARTFUL BLEND OF FORM AND FUNCTION. [RHAA]

Royston designed the vast majority of his parks for public agencies in the San Francisco Bay Area, but his first two ventures into park design were for private clients: Ladera Cooperative Housing near Palo Alto, and the Standard Oil Rod and Gun Club at Point Richmond, in the North Bay.

CHAPTER SIX

New Public Gardens: Case Studies, 1945–1965

LADERA COOPERATIVE HOUSING, 1945–1949

Garrett Eckbo received the commission for Ladera in 1945 and had completed some preliminary site analysis, but little design work. When Royston became a partner in Eckbo, Royston and Williams and agreed to head the San Francisco office, Eckbo delegated most of the responsibility for Ladera to him. Meanwhile, in 1946, Eckbo moved to Los Angeles to open a new office and assume responsibility for projects in that region.[115]

The Peninsula Housing Association, which commissioned the project, was critical of the shoddy, poorly planned suburban development typical of the Bay Area suburbs and wanted something better. The association envisioned "a democratic community" where individuals could "enjoy the advantages of country living, but without the high costs, isolation, and inconveniences we would face if we each tried

SITE PLAN
LADERA
PENINSULA HOUSING ASSOCIATION

SITE PLANNING BY
JOHN FUNK, GARRETT ECKBO, JOSEPH ALLEN STEIN
A R C H I T E C T S
JOHN FUNK, JOSEPH ALLEN STEIN
LANDSCAPE ARCHITECTS
E C K B O , R O Y S T O N & W I L L I A M S
CIVIL ENGINEER
N I C H O L A S   C I R I N O

54. *(OPPOSITE PAGE)* LADERA COOPERATIVE HOUSING, NEAR PALO ALTO, 1945–49. IN THIS PLAYGROUND DESIGN A CENTRAL WALK DIVIDES THE AREAS FOR PRESCHOOL AND OLDER CHILDREN. ORIGINALLY PUBLISHED IN ECKBO'S *LANDSCAPE FOR LIVING*. [EDA,UCB]

55. LADERA COOPERATIVE HOUSING. SITE PLAN. THE LANDSCAPE MATRIX CONNECTS ALL RESIDENCES WITH THE SCHOOL, THE RECREATION CENTER, THE COMMUNITY SHOPPING CENTER, AND THE PLAYGROUNDS. [EDA,UCB]

to go it alone."[116] This dream eventually dissolved in the acidic solution of the Federal Housing Authority loan policy, which denied the cooperative's request for a construction loan. The fact that Ladera was to be a racially integrated community may have been a major factor in the refusal.[117] By 1949, thirty-five houses had been constructed with individual financing, one house at a time, but that was all. That year the property sold to Eichler Homes, which developed part of the site following an alternative plan.

While the plan for Ladera remained mostly on paper, it is worth considering as an illustration of Royston's concept of a landscape matrix (figures 54, 55). Although Eckbo's role in the design details of the project may have been somewhat secondary, Ladera does display the conceptual overtones evident in Eckbo's earlier work for the Farm Security Administration (FSA) on communities for migrant workers and emergency World War II housing projects. It manifests a similar desire to create a community of clusters of housing units interwoven with a network of recreational spaces and essential service facilities.[118] Indeed, Eckbo and Royston may have collaborated on the design concept before Royston articulated its details. An additional influence on the plan was Royston's experience at Park Merced and other large-scale housing projects during the two years he was employed in the office of Thomas Church. With its centrally located elementary school, avoidance of through streets, and cul-de-sac arrangements, the plan also shares certain ideas from *Planning the Neighborhood*. A direct influence is unlikely, however, since this work was not published until 1948, when the design for Ladera was well underway.

Ladera was a collaborative effort with architects Joseph Allen Stein and John Funk and engineer Nicholas Cirino. Cirino had been employed by the FSA's San Francisco office, the same office Eckbo had worked in. Stein and Funk designed twelve different unit plans for the project, which featured the linkage of interior and exterior space on lots of different scales.

The program called for single-family houses for about four hundred families on a 260-acre site near Palo Alto. The site was challenging, hilly and split in half by a winding valley that made road alignment and house siting difficult. The terrain included a rolling plateau on the east side and a smaller, higher one in the northwest corner, accessible via a steep slope. From several points views opened to San Francisco Bay, and the valley was filled with numerous mature live oaks and native understory vegetation.

The design team responded to the site by laying down an armature of circulation that accessed the two plateaus, which provided the most suitable house sites. A loop road with twenty cul-de-sacs serves lots ranging from one-quarter to two-and-one-half acres. There is no through traffic, and the road system minimizes grading by careful alignment with the existing contours of the land. The curving valley itself is part of the landscape matrix, tying together the entire site plan. It functions as a linear park containing the major recreation facility of the site, a community center with swimming pools for adults and children, tennis courts, and a playground. Pedestrian paths run throughout the park, which remains in its natural state, and connect with the centrally located elementary school. Additional pedestrian paths, which form the rest of the matrix, link residences to the shopping center on the site's south perimeter. Most of these paths either run between the rear lot lines of the houses or skirt the circular turning areas of the cul-de-sacs. Thus one could visit friends, walk to school, drop by the recreation center, and shop for food without crossing a vehicular thoroughfare, a safety feature especially important for children.

Each cul-de-sac is given a distinct street tree planting to establish a unique identity, a device Eckbo had used in some of his previous FSA designs.[119] In addition, each cul-de-sac is in close proximity to one of the ten playgrounds for small children. Royston sites two larger playgrounds at the shopping center and recreation center. The smaller playgrounds tended to be simple rectangular designs that separated play areas for preschool children from those for older children. The two larger playgrounds are circular and divided into quadrants with more elaborate climbing apparatuses (see figure 54).[120]

The plan also includes a firehouse and restaurant next to the small shopping center as well as a kindergarten, guesthouse, and small interdenominational chapel. It clearly reflects the demographics of the rapidly developing Bay Area, with its numerous young families with small children. It is envisioned as a small village of about 1,600 people living as nuclear families with one or more children in single-family houses. They are to dwell in a "middle landscape," sharing the best of all residential worlds: rural living in the vicinity of large cities with all the advantages of culture and employment.[121] The whole is tied together by a park and connecting pedestrian paths— a first attempt at a landscape matrix.

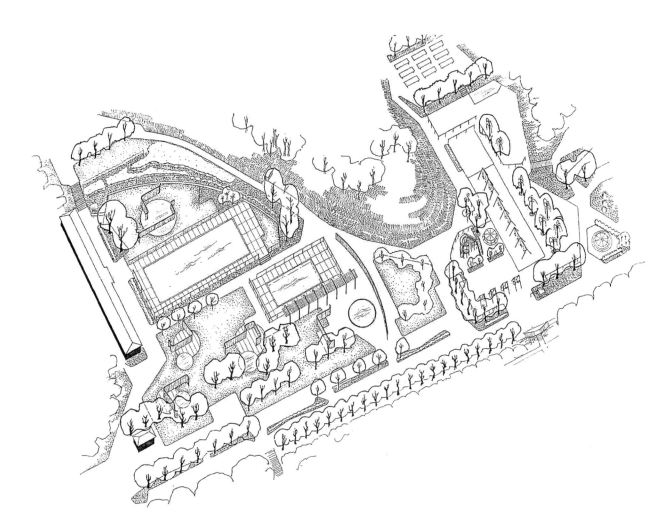

Royston was to pursue this ideal in future commissions and expand it to encompass an entire city; however, he was never able to achieve it in a large urban context.

THE STANDARD OIL ROD AND GUN CLUB, POINT RICHMOND, 1950

Royston's next major park commission was also in the private sphere. Unlike Ladera, this project was built and it attracted much favorable attention. His client was the Standard Oil Refinery (now the Chevron Refinery) at Point Richmond on the north shore of San Francisco Bay (figures 56, 57). The refinery's seven hundred employees had formed a club with facilities for fishing and skeet shooting and in 1950 wanted to expand it to include a wider range of recreational opportunities, especially for families with young children. The refinery workers shaped the park's program and did most of the construction themselves in their free time. They were pleased with the design, which attracted the attention of park executives and recreational planners throughout the Bay Area and was featured in the national journal *Parks and Recreation* and included in the 1958 exhibition of landscape architecture sponsored by the San Francisco Museum of Art.[122] At that time Royston's practice consisted mostly of residential com-

missions, and he welcomed the chance to design a park that would embody the spatial ideas and details of his smaller-scale projects (figure 58).

The approximately twenty-acre site was both promising and problematic. It fronted on the small cove with a beach providing long water views to the north. An encircling ridge of low hills with deep drainage swales formed the site's southern boundary. The hills were lush with mature coast live oaks (*Quercus agrifolia*) and other mature native vegetation, including California lilac (*Ceanothus*) and manzanita (*Arctostaphylos*). The amphitheater-like topography completely concealed any view of the large refinery, and the impression was one of an intimate harbor on a remote shore.

The frequent dense fogs and chilling north wind presented a problem typical of the varied microclimates in the Bay Area. One day Point Richmond might be foggy with a temperature of 60 degrees while the next it would be sunny and much warmer. Also, unlike Royston's later park sites, this one was no tabula rasa: already on the plot were a clubhouse, large gymnasium, and adult swimming pool, all of which, for economic reasons, were to be preserved. In addition, the program called for parking for some two hundred cars on the relatively small site.

56. STANDARD OIL ROD AND GUN CLUB, POINT RICHMOND, 1950. THIS STUDY PLAN ILLUSTRATES HOW THE TOPOGRAPHY WAS USED TO DEFINE THE SEPARATE RECREATION AREAS. [EDA, UCB]

57. STANDARD OIL ROD AND GUN CLUB. VIEW NORTH TOWARDS SAN FRANCISCO BAY. [EDA, UCB]

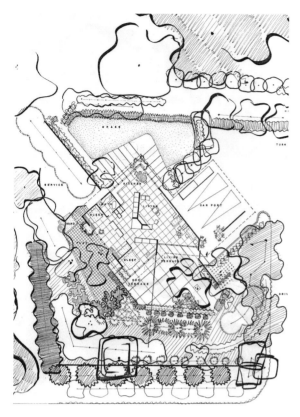

Royston skillfully uses the existing topography to create three distinct recreational zones linked by pedestrian paths (see figure 56). Two ridges project at right angles from the range of hills behind the park site and form three well-defined spatial pockets facing north on the Bay. The gymnasium already occupied the easternmost of these, and Royston reinforces its enclosure with a thick planting of trees. The center space holds the large adult swimming pool and to the west lies an open field. A straight road is located along the northern edge of the site, providing access to a beach, the old clubhouse, and a yacht basin farther west, which was not on refinery land.

A row of trees on either side of the road defines the park's entrance and connects its three main areas. A large parking lot on the western edge of the site frees the interior for pedestrians. Two new recreation zones catering to different age groups form the remainder of the park: a swimming area and a children's play area linked by a series of pedestrian walkways. These areas are sited in the middle and western precincts formed by the projecting ridges. Royston enlarges the swimming facilities by designing a preschool children's wading pool and an older children's swimming pool to supplement the existing adult facility (figure 59). Subtle level changes on the gently sloping site separate the pool areas and layer the park with a series of overlapping walls of trees and gracefully curving wooden screens that serve as windbreaks and suntraps for sunbathing (see figure 36). These screens resemble some of the fences in Royston's residential gardens, as do the lean steel and wooden pergolas that shade the seating areas near the pool (figure 60). A long, one-story building with dressing rooms forms a strong eastern boundary to the pool area. At the southern end of the site, at the base of the surrounding hills, densely shaded picnic areas offer quiet relief from the loud splashes and gleeful shouts of the pool areas. The construction materials throughout the park are durable and require little maintenance.[123] The ground plane in the sunbathing and pool areas is a mixture of turf and concrete slabs cast in irregularly shaped arcs and rectangles. Pergolas and play equipment are mostly made of bent and welded steel.

The play area in the westernmost spatial pocket contains some of Royston's early designs for imaginative play equipment. The centerpiece is a captivating twenty-five-foot-high spiral slide that Royston claims was for many years the tallest piece of play equipment in the Bay Area (figure 61).[124] Large revolving disks with centrifugal force that hurl gleeful children into a large sandbox,

58. ROYSTON GARDEN, MILL VALLEY, 1947. THE PLAN FOR ROYSTON'S OWN GARDEN SHOWS THE CLEAR SEPARATION OF USE AREAS, SIMILAR TO HIS PARK DESIGNS. [EDA,UCB]

59. STANDARD OIL ROD AND GUN CLUB, POINT RICHMOND, 1950. THE "POLLYWOG POOL" FOR PRE-SCHOOL CHILDREN, WITH THE HILLS BORDERING THE SITE CLEARLY VISIBLE. [RHAA]

60. STANDARD OIL ROD AND GUN CLUB. THE PERGOLA NEXT TO THE POOL IS A TYPICAL EXAMPLE OF AN OVER-SCALED RESIDENTIAL DESIGN DETAIL. [RHAA]

and a series of sculpture-like single and double swings add more excitement. The equipment is painted in bright colors and sturdily built by the refinery's skilled welders and metal workers, who worked free of charge on their holidays and weekends. The southern perimeter of the third zone also contains a picnic grove with barbecue pits that is separated by a thick buffer of trees from the large parking area to the west. Wall-like plantings in staggered rows layer this space as well, creating a visual impression of a larger space and making the park feel less crowded. Small, closely spaced, vertical wooden pickets surround the play area, dimensioned to allow parents or guardians to rest their elbows on the tops while supervising children's play, a typical example of Royston's emphasis on form dictated by human use. The planting plan for the entire site uses plants primarily to define spaces. Royston carefully preserves the existing large, native trees that formed shade canopies and plants the walkways with hardy, drought-resistant shrubs such as ceanothus, cistus, pyracantha, cytisus, and melaleuca for seasonal color and visually interesting textures.

Why did this park on private property in a remote section of the Bay Area attract so much attention? Zoned to avoid conflicting activities, it possessed a wide range of recreational

61. STANDARD OIL ROD AND GUN CLUB, POINT RICHMOND, 1950. THIS SLIDE—DESIGNED BY ROYSTON AND BUILT BY REFINERY EMPLOYEES—IS STILL IN USE AFTER HALF A CENTURY. [REUBEN RAINEY, 2003]

facilities for people of all ages. Its fresh spatial organization facilitated use while avoiding the appearance of the pretentious Beaux-Arts parks common in the prewar period, with their faux-Renaissance detailing and unimaginative recreational facilities. Royston's use of garden elements such as wooden fences and pergolas gave the park a feeling of familiarity and intimacy, almost as if the entire space were a larger residential patio with more elaborate play equipment. Its colorful and inventive custom-designed play apparatuses were a welcome change from the usual token swings and galvanized pipe contraptions typical of city parks, and its equipment and buildings were economical to build and easy to maintain. The purity of its geometry, its nonaxial spaces, and crisp understated details heralded new directions in the design vocabulary of American parks.

This highly functional yet elegant park—with its bold use of color and direct and creative response to program and site—exuded the can-do optimism of a prosperous, democratic nation entering a new era of peace and prosperity. As children splashed in the pools and friends gathered in the deep shade of the picnic area, a 1950s observer might well imagine a strain of Aaron Copeland's exuberant music resonating through the fresh North Bay air as an apt accompaniment to the lively scene.

KRUSI PARK, ALAMEDA, 1954

Pioneering design work often shocks and alienates before gaining acceptance; Royston's park at the Rod and Gun Club, however, was an instant success in the Bay Area. Park administrators from the city of Alameda, across the bay from San Francisco, visited it and came away wanting something similar for their own park system. They lacked a site as large, but they had available a small park adjacent to a kindergarten that served the local neighborhood of single-family, detached houses, a typical example of the prevailing "school-park" concept. Royston's highly original play equipment impressed them as they observed the children of the Standard Oil Refinery employees frolicking from one colorful apparatus to another. In 1954 they commissioned him to design a playground they christened "Tiny Tot Land" (figure 35). The playground catered to six-year-olds and under, and all children had to be accompanied by an adult. The park was open to children of the neighborhood as well as those attending the kindergarten. The design program resembled the recommendations in the 1956 *Guide for Planning Recreation Parks in California* and included a wading pool, sandbox, climbing apparatus, and an emphasis on wheeled toys such as small tricycles and pedal-cars.[125] The playground was an immediate success.

It elevated Royston's design of play equipment to a new level of sophistication and became the precedent for similar types of playgrounds sited in his larger parks of the 1950s and early 1960s, including Mitchell Park in Palo Alto and Central Park in Santa Clara.

The Krusi Park design commission challenged Royston to explore the nature of children's play in order to design apparatuses that would engage their fantasies as well as meet their need for a wide range of physical activities. The typical Bay Area children's playground of the early 1950s was a random assemblage of seesaws, swings, sandboxes, and galvanized pipe structures dubbed "monkey bars." The latter were a constant source of bruised knees, bumped heads, or worse. Since catalog products were almost nonexistent, park departments cobbled together equipment whose chief virtues were durability and low maintenance.

In rethinking his ideas on children's play, Royston examined his childhood memories and observed his own three children. He also studied how children used his new designs at the Rod and Gun Club. What he noted confirmed his belief that play is based on an innate predisposition for fantasy and adventurous physical activity involving some degree of risk. There is nothing particularly original

62. CHILDREN'S FAIRYLAND, OAKLAND. A LITERAL REPRESENTATION OF THE NURSERY RHYME "THERE WAS AN OLD WOMAN WHO LIVED IN A SHOE." [JC MILLER]

63. ROYSTON SPONTANEOUSLY SCRATCHING A WHIMSICAL CARTOON INTO WET CONCRETE AT ANOTHER PLAYGROUND UNDER CONSTRUCTION. ELDON BECK, A FUTURE PARTNER IN THE FIRM, LOOKS ON. UNIDENTIFIED SITE, NO DATE. [RHAA]

about this theory of play. What is significant was Royston's ability to embody it in his designs.

Furthermore, he was much opposed to more literal attempts to engage a child's fantasy by overt references to well-known figures from children's literature, film, and television. A typical example of this approach is Fairyland in nearby Oakland, where children encountered such giant figures as the Old Woman Who Lived in a Shoe and Snow White and the Seven Dwarfs in a veritable garden of literal images that talked when a key was inserted into a slot (figure 62).[126] Royston believes such literalness restricts a child's fantasy by confining it to a familiar set of media precedents. Instead, he prefers more abstract forms, free from predetermined associations, that would allow children to project their own fantasies onto them.[127] Thus, in a child's imagination, a row of sawed-off tree stumps that allowed her to jump from one to another could be a challenging route through the tops of trees high above the earth or an imaginary swamp filled with exotic creatures. His rejection of the literal is reminiscent of those who oppose figural sculpture in the design of memorials as too deterministic and restrictive of cultural memory.

The design for Krusi Park left most of the walks and tree-shaded lawn of the existing three-acre park intact and instead concentrated on the design of the playground, adjacent to the kindergarten building. In plan the design reads like a carefully composed abstract painting (see figure 35). Circular and semicircular forms play off against amoebic shapes layered on an irregularly gridded ground plane to create visual interest. A curvilinear 6-foot-high wall of wooden palings encloses the playground and separates it from the rest of the park. The fence is semitransparent, affording glimpses from without of the children at play and facilitating their supervision. Inwardly curving portions of the fence define its two welcoming entrances, a good example of line used to suggest movement through space—one of Royston's key design strategies.

Like the Rod and Gun Club park, the design is carefully zoned to accommodate children of different ages. The south end contains a cluster of circular play areas, a wading pool, a sand area, a playhouse that recalls the post-and-beam architecture of the surrounding suburbs, a shade trellis, a spiral slide, and a climbing structure for very small children. The sandbox's cleverly designed circular, stepped curb keeps sand in place. An inviting concrete play mountain rises from the center. Royston did no working drawing for the mountain. He met the construction crew the day of the pouring of the concrete and supervised the sculpting of its form (figure 63). The north end caters to older children and includes a colorful play sculpture composed of pipes designed by the artist Raymond Rice and a row of two-foot-high tree stumps to test a child's agility (figure 64). The main feature of this section is a large, freeway-like ramp for pedal-cars (figure 65). These are housed in a row of adjacent A-frame garages, which are locked at night. The ramp has a tight S-curve on the downgrade to test the skill of the more adventurous when they zoom down it, imitating their parents' attempts to negotiate the emerging freeway system of the Bay Area. A miniature gas station is located at the base of the ramp.

The playground materials are durable wood, steel, and concrete. Simple custom-designed benches and a few shade trees and pergolas accommodate the adults keeping watch over the children. Turf and sand cushion the falls of children in the play areas.

Krusi playground no longer exists, the victim, most likely, of reduced maintenance budgets and fears of litigation over its adventuresome play equipment. Surviving photographs and plans testify to Royston's attention to functional details combined with a mastery of playful sculptural form and clear spatial definition. Shortly after the completion of the playground

a kindergarten teacher remarked to Royston, "This is the only place around here where children don't cry."[128] This bit of well-meaning hyperbole pleased Royston, who certainly knew better, but the heavy use of the playground soon after completion did indeed testify to the design's success. In the 1958 exhibition of works of Bay Area landscape architecture sponsored by the San Francisco Museum of Art, it was described as "an experiment with imaginative space where wheel toys are the theme."[129] Ironically, it shared the same page in the catalog with Oakland's Fairyland, its polar opposite in playground design.

Krusi Park also provided a precedent for another sophisticated playground dating from the same year. Pixie Place, in Ross, embodied biocubic forms and original play structures, only fragments of which survive (figures 66, 67).

MITCHELL PARK, PALO ALTO, 1956

Royston's next major essay in park design, Mitchell Park in Palo Alto, synthesizes his earlier work at the Rod and Gun Club and Krusi Park (figure 68). It combines the functional zoning, layered spaces, and residential-scale details of the former with the fresh playground design of the latter (see figure 35). New to

64. *(OPPOSITE PAGE)* KRUSI PARK, ALAMEDA, 1954. VIVID COLORS ENHANCE THE PLAY SCULPTURE ADJACENT TO THE PEDAL-CAR FREEWAY. [RHAA]

65. KRUSI PARK. GASSING UP BEFORE ATTEMPTING THE FREEWAY. [RHAA]

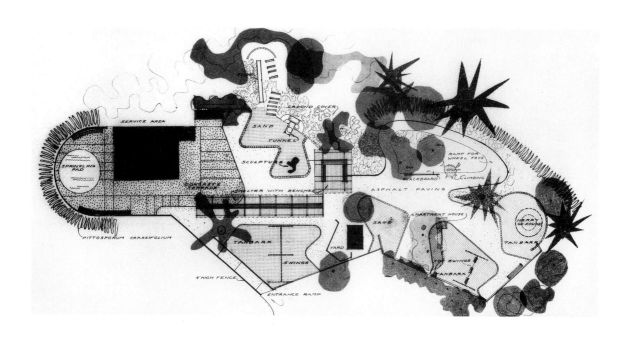

this synthesis are the sculpting of the ground plane to form a series of space-defining berms, a richer planting design palette, a perimeter treatment that affords views into the center of the park, more facilities for the elderly, a concrete circle that doubles as a stage and a roller-skating rink, and yet more innovative playground equipment. This is Royston's signature park; it attracted national attention in an article in *The American City*, a leading periodical for city officials, planners, and park administrators.[130] Delegates to the 1958 International Recreation Congress from Greece, Egypt, and Japan toured it, and the Palo Alto city planners praised it:

This park…establishes the pattern for the creative living theme. Novel ideas based on sound, practical recreation needs have emerged during the design and construction of this modern…recreational facility.[131]

The plan of the park published by the city as a user's guide listed twenty-nine features, including a wild garden, numerous picnic areas, playing fields, a community building, several children's playgrounds, and special facilities for the elderly, including lawn bowling (bocce), horseshoe pitches, and board-game tables (figure 69). It is one of the clearest embodiments of Royston's concept of a park as a public garden: it serves a wide range of age groups and creates a place for social gatherings and civic rituals that foster a sense of community. Unlike the Rod and Gun Club, which was on private land, its easily accessible site was very much in the public eye, which helped to spread its reputation.

After a visit to the Rod and Gun Club, Palo Alto officials invited Royston to design a park for an eighteen-acre site on the suburban fringe of the city. A flat site, once a wheatfield, it was adjacent to two new elementary schools and a middle school with about twelve acres for playgrounds and team sports. At that time Palo Alto planners embraced the idea suggested in *Planning the Neighborhood* of cellular neighborhoods centered on schools adjacent to parks. Meadow Park, as the park was initially named, was conceived as a large, citywide park intended to serve several "neighborhoods." Its name was changed to Mitchell Park just before its dedication on April 12, 1957, to honor J. Pearce Mitchell, a former professor at Stanford University and two-term mayor of Palo Alto who had also served on the city council for thirty-one years. The city council had the foresight to purchase land in a relatively undeveloped part of the city's suburban fringe before it became too expensive. The park site was acquired in 1952 for $69,724 with funds from a 1951 bond issue. Its total cost, including land acquisition,

66. PIXIE PLACE, ROSS, 1954. THE PIXIE PARK PLAN ECHOES THE BIOCUBIC FORMS AND CAREFUL ZONING OF KRUSI PARK. ROYSTON PROVIDED PRO-BONO DESIGN SERVICES FOR THIS PROJECT TO THE MARIN BRANCH OF THE AMERICAN ASSOCIATION OF UNIVERSITY WOMEN. [RHAA]

67. PIXIE PLACE. THE CHILDREN'S SPRAY POOL WAS ONE OF THE FIRST IN THE UNITED STATES. [RHAA]

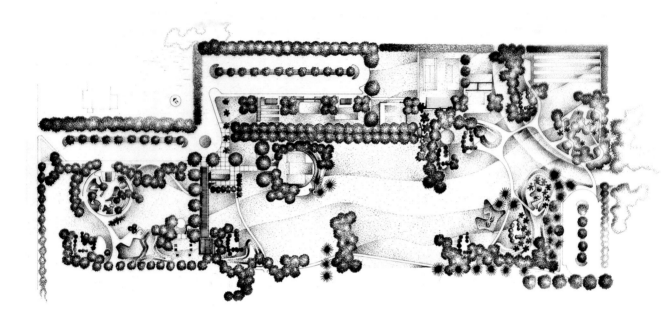

68. MITCHELL PARK, PALO ALTO, 1956. ONE OF THE BEST EXAMPLES OF ROYSTON'S CONCEPT OF A PARK AS A PUBLIC GARDEN. [EDA, UCB]

69. MITCHELL PARK. LEFT OF CENTER, THE COMMUNITY BUILDING. UPPER RIGHT, THE TINY TOT PLAYGROUND. NOTE THE DENSE DEVELOPMENT OF SINGLE FAMILY HOMES ON THE PARK'S BORDER. [RHAA]

70. MITCHELL PARK, PALO ALTO, 1956. PRESENTATION MODEL. IN THE FOREGROUND IS THE CIRCULAR TINY TOT PLAYGROUND. [RHAA]

71. *(BELOW LEFT)* MITCHELL PARK. THE MULTI-USE SLAB FUNCTIONS AS A THEATER AND A VENUE FOR GRADUATION CEREMONIES AND OTHER CELEBRATIONS. [NAT FARBER, EDA, UCB]

72. *(BELOW RIGHT)* MITCHELL PARK. ROLLER SKATING ON THE MULTI-USE SLAB. NOTE THE CUSTOM LIGHT FIXTURES DESIGNED EXCLUSIVELY FOR THIS PARK AND THE USE OF A BERM TO ENCLOSE THE SPACE. [RHAA]

construction, and designer's commission, was $293,982. Construction began in 1955.[132]

Royston drew upon his skills as a former actor when he presented his plan to a meeting of citizens and the city council. Several council members were skeptical of the need for a designer. One of the more vocal opponents noted that a few Boy Scouts scattering seeds around the old wheatfield could do the job for much less cost. At that point Royston entered the debate and requested permission to present his plan in more detail. This was granted, and Royston used a model (figure 70) and slides to outline the park's major features. After he finished, there was a moment of dead silence in the large gathering of citizens, then a burst of loud and sustained applause. His articulate and forceful presentation was the tipping point. The city council immediately voted approval.[133]

Royston himself designed almost all of Mitchell Park. During the early stages of the project, his partner Asa Hanamoto provided some insightful critiques. This was standard procedure for the San Francisco office of Eckbo, Royston and Williams, which in its early years assigned projects to individual designers.[134] Royston also consulted with Alex Smith, Palo Alto's director of parks and recreation. Smith too had a background in theater arts and suggested Royston include some sort of perform-

ance area in the park. He responded with a circular concrete slab, fifty-feet in diameter, with low seating walls that served as an amphitheater for musical performances and graduation ceremonies for the surrounding schools, as well as a roller skating rink (figures 71, 72). A colonnade of sycamore trees defined the edge of the multi-use slab (figure 73). Its surface was embellished with a pattern similar to several of the Mondrian-inspired patios he had designed earlier in the decade for residential clients (figure 74). A closer look at the pattern revealed that it incorporated the outline of a regulation badminton court. The original detailing of a backdrop with wings for the entry and exit of actors echoed the freestanding screens found in other areas of the park. About ten years after its completion, Royston worked with a local artist to remodel the backdrop, adding a colorful mural that recalled the paintings of Kandinsky.[135]

The eighteen-acre site formed a rectangle whose length was three-and-a-half times its width (see figure 68). In addition to the two elementary schools on its west border and the junior high on the south, a branch library to the east attracted more users to the site. The surrounding area was filling in rapidly with detached, single-family houses within easy walking distance.

A simple circulation system consisting of a single axis and a cross axis anchors the spaces within the park and gives easy access to its various parts. Gently curving turf berms define functional areas such as the playgrounds and theater and separate potentially conflicting activities (figure 75). When Royston learned that Palo Alto officials were trying to decide what to do with a surplus of soil excavated for a new sewer system, he persuaded them to haul it to the park site to create the berms. In addition, staggered, asymmetrical "walls" of trees and understory shrubs extend at right angles into the spacious central lawn (figure 76). These walls frame deep views that reach to the farthest boundaries, revealing the recreation areas. They also provide seasonal color, adding much needed variety to the long central space (see figure 44). The axis moving north to south is defined by the straight, tree-lined entry drive and parking area. It is conveniently sited near the small children's playground so parents needn't negotiate long distances. Royston transformed this axis into a walkway halfway into the park, after jogging it slightly to the east. The pedestrian axis terminates with a fountain and is flanked by an allée of mimosa trees (*Albizia julibrissin*), which provides shade and seasonal color. Adjacent to this axis and connected to it by a series of paths are facilities serving different

73. MITCHELL PARK, PALO ALTO, 1956. A COLONNADE OF SYCAMORES ARTICULATES THE EDGE OF THE MULTI-USE SLAB. THE WHEELCHAIR RAMP WAS ADDED IN 2004. [REUBEN RAINEY, 2006]

74. CHINN GARDEN, SAN FRANCISCO, 1950. THE COLORED CONCRETE PAVING PATTERN RESEMBLES THE ORIGINAL SURFACE TREATMENT OF MITCHELL PARK'S MULTI-USE SLAB. IN FIGURE 40 THE SLAB'S PATTERN IS VISIBLE ON THE MODEL OF THE PARK, JUST LEFT OF CENTER. [RHAA]

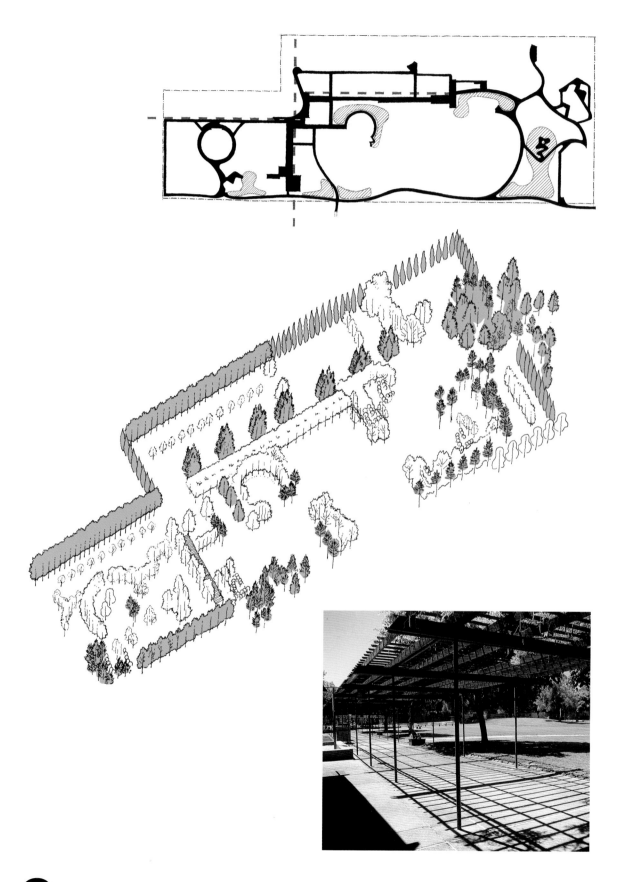

age groups—a tiny tot area, a shuffleboard court, bocce court, paddle tennis area, and tennis practice area. Across a channelized creek in the southeast corner of the park a wild garden composed of redwood trees and thick understory shrubs offers a quiet retreat. Also, tucked into the far southeast corner of the park is a small archery range, carefully sited to keep this potentially dangerous activity far from the other areas.

The other major portion of the circulation system, the east-west cross axis, forms a junction with the north-south one near a small, one-story, multi-use building. This includes a meeting room for community functions, a "teen lounge" and patio, and the office of the recreation supervisor, who coordinates team sports and various other group activities of the older children, such as archery and art classes. This cross axis extends westerly along a concrete walkway covered with a wisteria arbor (figure 77). It terminates at the senior citizens' area, where there are horseshoe pitches, chess tables, a picnic area, and a putting green. Royston employs five-foot turf-covered berms to separate the children's play area from the senior citizens' facilities and to screen a parking area at the south end of the park. Berms of three feet enclose the tiny-tot playground and the circular amphi-

theater to the south. The twelve acres of the junior high playing fields to the west, which are not officially a part of the park, remain in full view. They join the park's boundary seamlessly and share the same turf ground plane. This strategy of borrowed views makes the eighteen-acre park appear much larger. A circuit walk on the perimeter opens onto a series of interesting vistas with opportunities for strollers to observe the activities within.

Family picnic areas in small, room-like spaces defined by a combination of hedges and wooden screens for privacy occupy several sites in the park as do a series of children's playgrounds (figure 78). The main tiny tot area, with its strong biocubic forms, included some of Royston's most imaginative play equipment, all of which displayed his careful blending of form with function (figure 79). "The apartment house," a multistory structure of stacked wire-mesh cubes connected by a ladder, was very popular with children although perhaps less beloved of parents who occasionally had to climb the twelve-foot-high tower to retrieve their progeny (figure 80). This structure allowed children to experience height without fear of falling or need for parental supervision. Royston believes that certain sensations, such as surprise, height, free movement, and concealment, are important

75. MITCHELL PARK, PALO ALTO, 1956. CIRCULATION DIAGRAM AND LOCATION OF BERMS. THE HATCHED AREAS INDICATE EARTH BERMS, AND THE RED DASHES, THE TWO PRINCIPAL AXES. [EMMANUEL DIDIER]

76. MITCHELL PARK. THE PLANTING PLAN ILLUSTRATES ROYSTON'S USE OF PLANTS TO STRUCTURE SPACE. EVERGREEN TREES DEFINE THE PARK'S EDGE. [EMMANUEL DIDIER]

77. MITCHELL PARK. THE 150-FOOT LONG PERGOLA DEFINES THE EAST-WEST CROSS AXIS. [MARC TREIB, 2004]

78. MITCHELL PARK, PALO ALTO, 1956. ROYSTON'S STUDY SKETCH OF A PROPOSED FAMILY PICNIC AREA. THE WOODEN FENCES IN THE BACK-GROUND WERE INTENDED TO PROVIDE PRIVACY UNTIL THE HEDGES MATURED. [EDA, UCB]

79. MITCHELL PARK. AXONOMETRIC STUDY PLAN FOR THE TINY TOT PLAYGROUND. THE BIOCUBIC FORMS ARE ZONED IN A RADIAL PATTERN AND SCALED TO VARIOUS PLAY ACTIVITIES. [RHAA]

80. *(OPPOSITE PAGE)* MITCHELL PARK. THE "APARTMENT HOUSE," A HIGH-RISE CLIMBING STRUCTURE AND SLIDE. [RHAA]

parts of a child's development and designed many of his play structures to evoke them. The biomorphic wading pool was another favorite spot. Scaled to the reach of a parent's voice, the depth decreased as a child moved away from the edge toward its center, farther from adult assistance (figure 81). The "gopher holes," cut into a hollow, curving, concrete slab set into a turf berm were another especially popular feature (figure 82). This structure invited children to disappear underground and pop up elsewhere like so many energetic woodchucks, accommodating their need for both concealment and surprise. Royston also included a freeway with pedal-cars, complete with garages and a gas station (figure 83). The local fire department kept the pedal-cars in working order and locked them in their garages at night. This freeway was somewhat tamer than the one in Krusi Park since it lacked a steep ramp. In addition to climbing bars and swings, the playground featured Bay Area artist Virginia Green's two large concrete sculptures of bears, whose lightly textured surfaces were designed to invite climbing (figure 84).[136]

The vegetation design for Mitchell Park uses plants primarily to define space and to call attention to seasonal change (figure 85). As noted, allées of trees mark the north-south axis, while a wisteria pergola clearly articulates the east-west one. Trees planted inside the hedge walls of picnic areas create low ceilings, welcome shade, and a feeling of intimacy. Royston paid special attention to leaf textures and growth habit when selecting the large-scale trees for the park. Red-flowering horse chestnuts (*Aesculus* x *carnea*), which formed one of the walls that extended into the park, were chosen for their large-sized leaves, horizontal branching pattern, and seasonal color. Highly textured evergreen trees such as Hollywood junipers contribute additional visual interest (see figure 43). The planting consists mostly of trees and low maintenance shrubs and turf but is notable for the variety of species. Indeed, Mitchell Park is among the more gardenesque of Royston's public gardens, second only to Bowden Park, its neighbor about a mile to the north. Specimen stone pines (*Pinus pinea*) offer additional shade in Palo Alto's hot, dry summer climate—a far cry from the cool, fog-drenched climate of the North Bay site of the Rod and Gun Club (figure 86). Redwood groves define the picnic area in the northwest corner of the park and add interest to the quiet sanctuary of the wild garden at the park's opposite end.

However, the lack of existing vegetation on the old wheatfield site presented a problem. Newly planted trees and shrubs would not

81. *(OPPOSITE PAGE ABOVE)* MITCHELL PARK, PALO ALTO, 1956. THE WIDTH OF THE WADING POOL WAS DETERMINED BY THE REACH OF A GUARDIAN'S VOICE. [RHAA]

82. *(OPPOSITE PAGE BELOW)* MITCHELL PARK. "GOPHER HOLES." [RHAA]

83. MITCHELL PARK. THIS PEDAL-CAR FREEWAY WAS SOMEWHAT TAMER THAN THE ONE BUILT AT KRUSI PARK. [RHAA]

84. MITCHELL PARK. ARTIST VIRGINIA GREEN'S FROLICKING BEAR SCULPTURES. [RHAA]

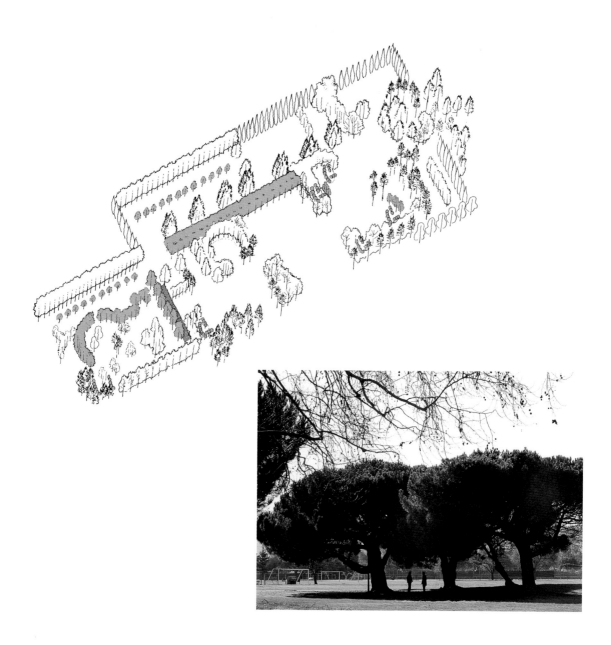

define spaces effectively until they matured years later. The berms helped to address this problem, but Royston also employed a series of six-foot high curving fences in the senior citizens' area, the tiny-tot area, and the picnic spaces. These, like the fences at the Rod and Gun Club, created immediate spatial definition, which was reinforced by the plants as they matured. Pergolas carefully positioned to cast dramatic shadow patterns on the walks are painted in one of Royston's favorite colors, Chinese red (figure 87). The lighting and seating are also custom designed. Royston followed this procedure in most of his later parks, giving each its own ambiance and individual character by avoiding repetition of details used previously.[137]

The design vocabulary of Mitchell Park raises an interesting question: What occurs visually when biocubic forms applied successfully to small-scale residential gardens are adapted to a larger park? Can park users experience, or "read," such forms, or are they indecipherable in a larger space experienced sequentially rather than taken in at a single glance? Royston was conscious of this issue and dealt with it successfully. The smaller playground areas of Mitchell Park express a rich array of biocubic forms that are readily perceived since these spaces are about the size of a large residential garden. However, he realized that the larger, meadow-like center of the park demanded a different approach. His tree walls—a far simpler treatment widely spaced at irregular intervals—read clearly and create a sense of a free-flowing spatial continuum down the center of the park, tying together its various areas (see figure 68). If echoes of Kandinsky's complexity appear in the playgrounds, reverberations of Mies van der Rohe's clarity are present in the central meadow.[138]

As previously noted, the scale and program of the park bore a striking resemblance to the recommendations for a community recreation park contained in the *Guide for Planning Recreation Parks in California*. For example, this study prescribed that such a park be a minimum of 32.75 acres. Mitchell Park, designed to serve several neighborhoods, is about 30 acres including the pre-existing school athletic fields. The study also called for "a concrete slab for skating and dancing," a "community center building," and additional features such as "a wheel-toy freeway," "gopher holes," and "play sculptures," all of which appear in Mitchell Park.[139] The *Guide* was published in 1956, one year before Mitchell Park was dedicated. Royston does not recall consulting it for programmatic ideas, but the

85. MITCHELL PARK, PALO ALTO, 1956. IN ROYSTON'S PLANTING PLAN EVERGREENS MAINTAIN THE PARK'S SPATIAL DEFINITION THROUGHOUT THE YEAR WHILE SPRING BLOOM CELEBRATES SEASONAL CHANGE AND HIGHLIGHTS THE PRINCIPAL AXES. [EMMANUEL DIDIER]

86. MITCHELL PARK. STONE PINES ADJACENT TO THE PRIMARY LAWN SPACE OFFER MUCH-NEEDED SHADE DURING THE SUMMER MONTHS. [REUBEN RAINEY, 2006]

87. MITCHELL PARK. THE "CHINESE RED" PERGOLA IN THE SENIOR CITIZENS' AREA. [REUBEN RAINEY, 2004]

close resemblance is indeed striking. As pre-viously noted, these similarities probably stem from Royston's recommending such details to the committee formulating the study in response to its questionnaire. Many offices throughout California had received such questionnaires. Apparently the committee liked Royston's ideas and included many of them in the publication.[140]

While Royston's design shares programmatic similarities to the state-sponsored study, it is clear that his work goes well beyond it. The zone diagrams published in the study locate functions such as picnicking and playgrounds in a single area (figure 27).[141] In Mitchell Park picnic areas and playgrounds are more widely distributed, thus avoiding the monotony of single-use zones and inviting users to explore the park's full extent. Also, the diagrams did not specify a particular design vocabulary. They could have been realized with an axial Beaux-Arts scheme detailed to resemble a seventeenth-century French chateau garden or a sixteenth-century Italian Renaissance villa. Royston's interlocking spaces and striking biocubic forms transcend anything suggested by the study. The Palo Alto planners working with Royston recognized this and characterized his work as "novel," "modern," and "embody-ing the creative living theme."[142]

Mitchell Park remains one of Royston's favorite design projects, along with the Rod and Gun Club, Krusi Park, and Santa Clara's Central Park. He regards it as both a sophisticated culmination of his first decade of park work and a point of departure for further design odysseys.

BOWDEN PARK, PALO ALTO, 1960

Successful projects often pose a temptation to repeat them. Royston's design for the Jeffrey Bowden Park demonstrates that he avoided that ever-beckoning path to stagnation and mediocrity by creating something new while restating effective elements of his previous designs. In the planning taxonomy of its day Bowden Park was classified as a "neighborhood park." The three-acre park is one of Royston's smallest and most garden-like in the literal sense. It is essentially a rectangular stroll garden with a display of ornamental plants, a small playground at one end, and a swath of lawn down the middle. Royston termed it a "visual space" as well as a "play area." Its special emphasis on ornamental plants is unique among Royston's parks (figure 88).[143]

The park is located across from a commuter rail station and faces a busy six-lane boulevard to its west. Its south end abuts a major four-

88. BOWDEN PARK, PALO ALTO, 1960. THE CONSISTENT RECTILINEAR GEOMETRY OF THE PLAN IS UNIQUE AMONG ROYSTON'S PARKS, AS IS ITS EXTENSIVE USE OF ORNAMENTAL PLANTS. [RHAA]

89. BOWDEN PARK, 1960. TAI CHI PRACTITIONERS ON THE CENTRAL LAWN. [MARC TREIB, 2004]

lane underpass. The north perimeter is a somewhat less travelled thoroughfare, while the eastern side borders on a quiet suburban neighborhood of detached single-family houses. Thus the park forms a bridge between the hectic pace of the workaday world and the calmer life of the suburbs. Prior to Royston's involvement, the park offered the public little beyond a flat, patchy lawn with some typically unimaginative galvanized steel play equipment. Commuters lobbied city officials to convert the site into a parking lot serving the rail station. The city manager resisted that suggestion and instead called in Royston to create a new park.

In his design concept, based upon the prevailing nuclear family concept of the time that underlay such works as *Planning the Neighborhood*, Royston recognized the site's role as a threshold and envisioned the park primarily as a place where wives could bring their young children and meet their husbands returning home from their daily commutes. Returning husbands and their wives could share a quiet, restorative stroll in the public garden while the children played in the small playground. Parents and children could also casually interact with other families before walking home, having experienced the spontaneous friendly encounters that foster a strong sense of neighborhood identity. The fact that

the park was originally based on a now-outdated notion of the nuclear family and suburban planning has, however, not resulted in a sociological dinosaur. Today the park continues to be heavily used by the neighborhood and retains essentially the same facilities. Now stay-at-home fathers may be the ones waiting for their wives or partners to return from work; unmarried couples may use it in a similar fashion; and Tai Chi, Chi Gong, martial arts, and Sufi meditation may at times replace croquet or kickball as a more multicultural community has developed in the Palo Alto suburbs (figure 89). Yet recent conversations with its users reveal that the park continues to foster a sense of neighborhood in a social context much altered from the 1960s.[144]

The design of the rectangular site with its north-south orientation employed formal strategies Royston had developed previously in Mitchell Park as well as some ideas adapted from his residential gardens, especially the Mondrian-like rectilinear geometry of the 1950 Chinn Garden (see figure 74). To add interest to the flat topography and to create the illusion of greater extent, Royston sited one five-foot-high berm near the park's southern edge and another adjacent to the playground near the northern boundary. The south berm blocked a view to the busy four-lane underpass and supplied a hill for children to roll down. The north berm was capped by a cubical log shelter reminiscent of the Bay Area's Arts-and-Crafts architectural tradition (figures 90, 91). The earthforms afforded easy monitoring of children playing on the large central lawn. Royston also preserved a large oak at the south end of the site as an attractive counterpoint to the log shelter.[145]

The plan subtly contrasts symmetry and asymmetry. A perimeter walk frames the entire site. Attached to this walk on the long sides is a series of rectilinear beds planted with low-growing shrubs of varying colors, textures, and heights. For the interior beds Royston specified groundcovers with colorful flower accents such as gazania and pelargonium. On the street side of the park a plant popular in the period, Hahn's ivy (*Hedera helix* 'Hahni'), defines the planting beds.[146] Paved areas with benches articulate the beds at regular intervals, and the entire composition creates a rich and colorful geometrical pattern reminiscent of a Mondrian painting (figure 92). The combination of planting and paving takes on the appearance of a large parterre and is especially visible from atop the berms at each end. This is another excellent example of Royston's ability to apply a residential design vocabulary to a small park

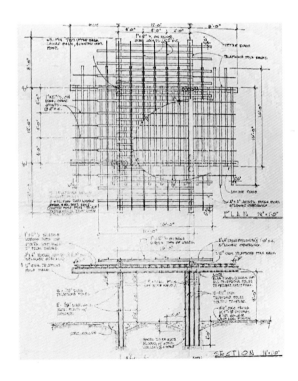

90. BOWDEN PARK, PALO ALTO, 1960. THE LOG PAVILION IS THE FIRST EXPRESSION OF THE MORE RUSTIC VOCABULARY ROYSTON EMPLOYS IN HIS LATER WORK. NOTE THE CAPPED CONCRETE PIPE SEATS. [RHAA]

91. BOWDEN PARK. CONSTRUCTION DRAWING FOR THE LOG PAVILION. A TYPICAL EXAMPLE OF CAREFUL ATTENTION TO DETAIL. [RHAA]

that can be viewed as a whole from a single vantage point. The entire pattern of the ground plane is bilaterally symmetrical and is boldly accented by the varying plant textures played off against alternating squares of decomposed granite and concrete. Low boxwood hedges (*Buxus microphylla* var. *japonica*) enclose the bench areas and give a sense of privacy (figure 93). Double rows of trees along the east edge (*Pistacia chinensis*) screen a parking lot. Another double row (*Liquidambar styraciflua*, sweetgum) on the west boundary buffers the busy six-lane thoroughfare. Deciduous trees add considerably to visitors' comfort, offering dappled shade in summer and allowing sunshine to warm seating areas in winter. The varied fall color of both species adds visual interest.

The large central turf area accommodates many activities such as lounging, martial arts, and small-scale lawn sports like badminton and croquet. A series of asymmetrical, low hedges set at right angles to the central lawn overlays the strong geometry of the bilaterally symmetrical walk and planting-bed composition. These overlapping hedges offer some welcome visual tension by playing off against the walk and planting-bed configurations. At both ends of the park, groves of umbrella-like Mediterranean stone pines (*Pinus pinea*) shade picnic areas and create places for quiet repose. These dark evergreens are balanced by a stand of twelve silvery-blue mountain gums (*Eucalyptus pulverulenta*) and linear plantings of graceful trees such as golden willow (*Salix babylonica* 'Aurea') and lemon bottlebrush (*Calistemon citrinus*). Accent trees with strong forms, such as Irish yew (*Taxus baccata* 'Stricta') and Hollywood juniper (*Juniperus chinensis* var. *tortulosa*) complete this painterly composition.

With a nod toward economy Royston specified cut and capped concrete sewer pipes as stools for the picnic tables (see figure 90). The custom benches and light standards designed for Mitchell Park reappear at Bowden (figure 94), a rare exception to his usual practice of creating different details for each of his parks. Budget constraints dictated a smaller and simpler children's play area than those in Mitchell or Krusi Parks. In this playground Royston built climbing bars, swings, seesaws, and slides of bent-pipe, several quite whimsical, resembling people and giant toadstools (figure 95). Because the playground was skillfully sited next to the underground passage to the rail station, returning commuters could easily greet their children and spouses.

Bowden Park is a mid-twentieth-century version of a parterre garden. Unlike a seventeenth-century French parterre, however, its pattern

92. BOWDEN PARK, PALO ALTO, 1960. A DETAIL OF THE PLANTING PLAN ILLUSTRATES THE WIDE VARIETY OF SPECIES DESIGNATED FOR THE ORIGINAL FLOWER BEDS. [RHAA]

93. BOWDEN PARK. MATURE HEDGES ENCLOSE THE BENCHES ALONG THE PERIMETER WALK, OFFERING A SENSE OF PRIVACY TO PARK VISITORS. [REUBEN RAINEY, 2006]

94. BOWDEN PARK. THE CUSTOM-MADE BENCHES AND LIGHT FIXTURES ARE IDENTICAL TO THOSE USED IN MITCHELL PARK. [RHAA]

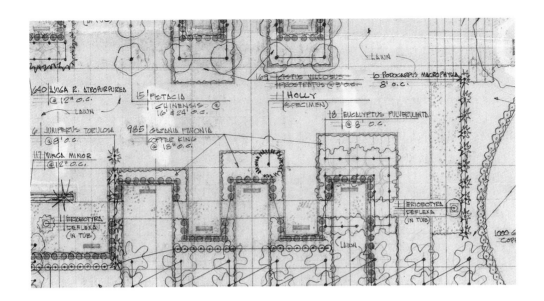

derives from the asymmetry of avant-garde painting rather than the elaborate embroidery of aristocratic garments. And unlike a traditional parterre, the park site is not simply to be viewed; it is a space for play and quiet contemplation. By calling it a "visual space" Royston meant it was designed to evoke "a sense of wonder at the beauty of plants."[147]

In its capacity as a neighborhood park, Bowden was designed to strengthen community ties in a region where the average family in the exploding suburban fringe may move as often as every five years. Royston's fresh intepretation of a parterre garden in a twentieth-century democratic society echoed the teaching of his former professor H. Leland Vaughan, who encouraged creative use of historical precedent.

CENTRAL PARK, SANTA CLARA, 1960–1975

Central Park remains the grand synthesis of Royston's ideas about park design during the 1950s. If we were to regard the Rod and Gun Club as a concerto, Krusi Park, a minuet, and Mitchell Park as a later, more nuanced concerto, then Central Park is Royston's symphony. At 52 acres, it is his largest park and contains some of his most sophisticated planting design, spatial organization, and accommodations for park users (figure 96). The basic design

95. BOWDEN PARK, PALO ALTO, 1960. THE HEIGHT OF THE PLAYGROUND FENCES ALLOWS PARENTS TO LEAN COMFORTABLY ON THEIR ELBOWS AS THEY OBSERVE THEIR CHILDREN AT PLAY. THE PLAY EQUIPMENT IS CUSTOM DESIGNED. [RHAA]

of the park was expressed in its 1960 plan. However, construction was phased in seventeen discrete stages and not completed until the mid-1970s; nonetheless, during this fifteen-year period only a few minor alterations modified the original plan.

Central Park marks a turning point in Royston's design method in that it was a more collaborative effort. Royston formulated the master plan and many of the design details, after which his partners Asa Hanamoto, Kaz Abey, Louis Alley, Pat Carlisle, and Harold Kobayashi developed and refined various elements (see figure 15).[148]

During the 1950s, Santa Clara's suburbs were among the fastest growing in the Bay Area. Located in the rich alluvial soils of the southern portion of San Francisco Bay, until World War II the city was completely surrounded by fruit orchards and truck gardens, and its economy depended mostly on the processing of agricultural products. From 1950 to 1959 it doubled in land area while its population quadrupled. This was a young population typical of many of the smaller Bay Area cities, with an average age of 28.2 and 29 percent under the age of 15. As its economy shifted to high tech industries Santa Clara became a wealthy city with the third highest income of Bay Area cities of comparable size. Its city planners, like those

of Palo Alto, adopted the neighborhood strategy of *Planning the Neighborhood* to bring order to growth, and their proposals included a system of clearly delineated park types. Its young, relatively well-to-do inhabitants demanded that this system be first-rate, and its elected officials responded with a master plan and bond issue to expand the park and recreation system from a meager 45 acres to 711 acres.[149]

The city's director of parks and recreation was Earl Carmichael, an energetic visionary and skilled lobbyist. His regime belonged to an era when citizen reviews and environmental impact statements were almost nonexistent. A charismatic figure like Carmichael could implement a park system through personal contacts and direct lobbying with city officials, nearly free of constraints.[150]

Carmichael had visited the Rod and Gun Club, Krusi Park, and Mitchell Park and was determined to have the likes of them for his city. Before construction funds had been appropriated, he commissioned Royston to design Central Park, the largest of the city's projected public landscapes. He then gathered support for the design and persuaded city officials to initiate a bond issue to fund it and other small neighborhood parks. The citizens of Santa Clara passed the initiative by a large majority. After this initial success Carmichael and

Royston collaborated for about fifteen years to produce numerous neighborhood parks and a civic plaza park for Santa Clara.[151] Carmichael and Royston's respect for one another's professionalism and their shared vision for the potential of parks to enrich a community soon developed into a personal friendship.[152]

Their collaboration was quite effective in gaining support for new parks. Unlike in Palo Alto and elsewhere, Royston did not present his own designs at city council meetings. Carmichael handled this part of the process, presenting the plans after he had already engaged in considerable lobbying with individual city officials and council members. In the case of Central Park, Carmichael had Royston build a large-scale model of it, which he then placed in the center of the lobby of city hall where officials passed every day. So impressed were they by the design that they quickly introduced the bond proposal to fund the new park system. Royston's model continued to be useful throughout the park's fifteen-year phased construction, keeping before the eyes of city officials the original vision of the park, lest they be tempted to compromise it with ill-conceived cost cutting.[153]

Carmichael was also very wise in his long-range planning. His agency bought parkland long before construction funding was available and before rapidly expanding suburbs made it astronomically expensive. Central Park's 52 acres was one of these far-sighted acquisitions. Royston's only disappointment in working with Carmichael was that he never persuaded him to create a true landscape matrix, which would have consisted of a system of parks connected by bike paths and trails along the numerous city creeks that drained into the Bay. (Carmichael thought the occasional flooding of the creeks during the winter rainy season rendered them too dangerous as recreation areas.) However, Royston did persuade him to support an extensive, citywide tree-planting program, which in Royston's view was an important first step in creating an interconnected series of green spaces that would inject much-needed order and amenity into the city's rapid growth.[154]

Central Park's site, purchased at a cost of $700,000 in 1959, was flat and blessed with rich alluvial soil—it had once been a productive fruit orchard.[155] The boundaries of the site formed an irregular polygon, bordered on its west and south by major thoroughfares. Saratoga Creek sliced across the park northeast to southwest in a deep swale, clearly dividing the park into two sections. Adjacent to the north boundary was an elementary school, while detached single-family houses surrounded the rest of the park.

The site plan incorporated typical Royston features—clear zoning of functional areas, a strong spatial organization, a rich and varied planting plan, sculptural treatment of the ground plane using berms, a wide range of imaginative features for all age groups, and design details reminiscent of residential gardens (figure 97).

The first part to be completed was east of Saratoga Creek where Royston sited a large public library, a massive international swim center with multiple pools and bleachers for 5,500, a baseball stadium, a children's zoo, and a tennis complex along the eastern border (figure 98). A straight access road connects these features and accommodates ample curbside parking. With the exception of the children's zoo, all of these facilities were realized. Restricting automobiles almost exclusively to the park's eastern and southern edges allows the rest of the site to function as an auto-free pedestrian area given over to strolling, picnicking, playgrounds, and small theatrical events.

A well-defined center consisting of a two-acre lake adjacent to a large, tent-like picnic pavilion borders on two "meadow" areas on either side of Saratoga Creek (figure 99). Gently curving pedestrian paths reach out from the picnic structure like slender arms embracing the meadows, providing a promenade of ever-changing views and expanding and contracting space defined by gentle berms. The main path system eventually circles back to its point of origin and along the way its branches connect with the numerous sports facilities on the eastern perimeter (see figure 97).

The tall, circular picnic pavilion looms over the park like a festive circus tent. It is both playful and monumental (figure 100). Given its height, equivalent to a seven-story building, it orients park users and serves as a community gathering place for families and citizens' groups. Functioning as a kind of covered piazza, it is another of Royston's devices intended to nurture community bonds. This huge picnic tent—a unique venture into civic monumentality—bears a remote resemblance to much smaller structures in his residential garden designs (see figure 47). Its circular base is 160 feet in diameter, and in its center is a 75-foot-high steel column from which a series of galvanized chains are suspended to form the canopy. Originally wisteria vines were intended to grow along the full length of the chains to create a dense green canopy. However, for reasons of maintenance the wisteria is allowed to grow only about a third of the way up the chains. This opens the central turf area to the sun, a modification that Royston welcomed since it offers users a choice of sun

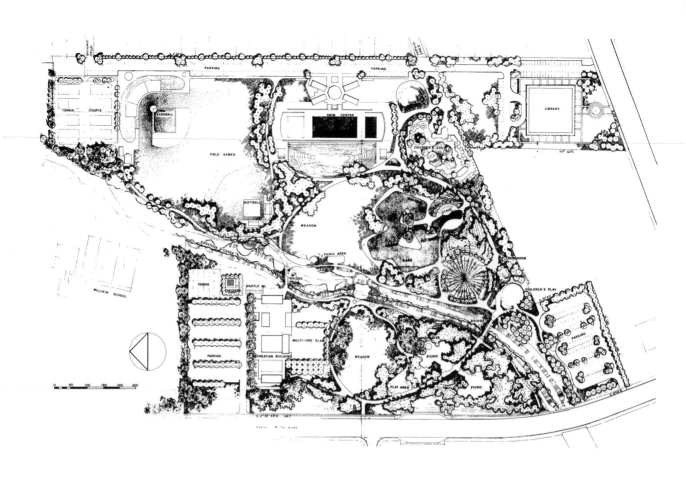

96. CENTRAL PARK, SANTA CLARA, 1960–75. SITE PLAN, 1960. CONSTRUCTED IN PHASES OVER FIFTEEN YEARS, THIS WAS THE LARGEST AND MOST COMPLEX PARK OF ROYSTON'S EARLY CAREER. [RHAA]

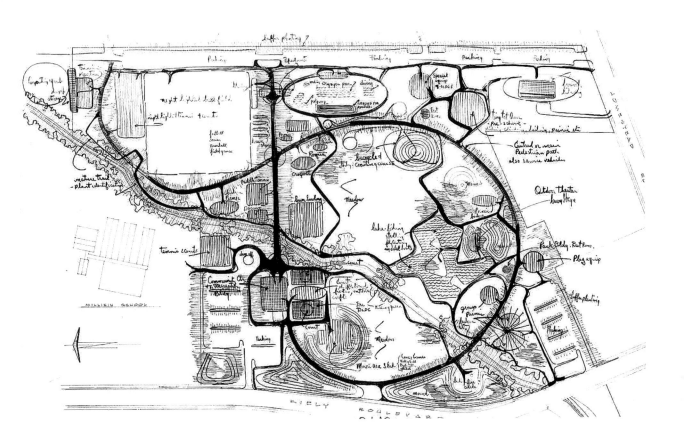

97. CENTRAL PARK, SANTA CLARA, 1960–75. A ZONING AND CIRCULATION DIAGRAM OF THE PARK. EARTH BERMS DEFINE VARIOUS RECREATION AREAS. [RHAA]

98. CENTRAL PARK. THE INTERNATIONAL SWIM CENTER IN ITS INITIAL PHASE. TODAY'S BLEACHERS ARE MUCH LARGER AND INCLUDE AN ALL-WEATHER COVER. ROYSTON ALSO DESIGNED THE DIVING PLATFORM. [RHAA]

99. CENTRAL PARK, SANTA CLARA, 1960–75. THE TENT-LIKE PICNIC PAVILION AND NEARBY LAKE DEFINE THE PARK'S CENTER. THE BAYS OF THE LAKE ACCOMMODATE DIFFERENT RECREATIONAL ACTIVITIES, SUCH AS MODEL BOATING AND FLYCASTING. IN THE UPPER RIGHT, THE INTERNATIONAL SWIM CENTER IS BARELY VISIBLE. [RHAA]

100. CENTRAL PARK, SANTA CLARA, 1960–75. THE SEVENTY-FIVE-FOOT-HIGH SUPPORT POLE FOR THE PAVILION CANOPY SERVES AS A LANDMARK. WISTERIA VINES EMBELLISH THE PERIMETER OF THE STRUCTURE AND CREATE WELCOME SUMMER SHADE. [MARC TREIB, 2004]

101. CENTRAL PARK. THE RUSTIC PICNIC PERGOLA IN THE WEST AREA OF THE PARK. [RHAA]

102. CENTRAL PARK. THE FOUNTAIN JET IN THE CENTRAL LAKE AERATES THE WATER AND ANIMATES THE SCENE. THE RUSTIC STONE WALLS FOR SEATING ARE CHARACTERISTIC OF PARKS DESIGNED BY THE ROYSTON FIRM IN THE 1970s AND 1980s. [RHAA]

or shade (figure 100). A raised terrace circles the perimeter and contains picnic tables, large barbecue grills, tables for food layout, and sinks for clean up.[156] A small playground for young children is located conveniently near the picnic tent, which is served by a parking lot on the south edge of the park. This picnic facility proved so popular that several years later a similar one was developed in the west area of the park. This one is less monumental, with detailing more like a circular wooden pergola in a residential garden (figure 101). The circular log posts recall the timber pavilion in Bowden Park, but in this instance the structure is focused inward, defining and enclosing a large circular space.[157]

The two-acre lake at Central Park takes the form of an irregular polygon articulated with a series of bays zoned for specific activities such as flycasting contests, model boating, and fishing (see figure 99). The lake is divided into two levels connected by a low waterfall, which aerates the water and creates a pleasant murmur. Two large spray fountains supply additional aeration and visual interest while large stone cobbles rim the lake, providing erosion control as well as an accent of bold texture (figure 102).[158] Across Saratoga Creek is one of Royston's most original playground designs. Large, cube-shaped granite blocks

with hollow circular cores form a series of climbing mazes (figure 103). Royston discovered the raw material for this playground when visiting a quarry that had kept the hollowed-out cores of blocks cut for the columns of San Francisco's City Hall. A sculptor added some rough texture to their sides, and Royston integrated them with swings and slides to form a play space that continues to delight children.

Central Park's planting plan is one of the most elaborate of any of Royston's public landscapes of the 1950s. Groves of redwood trees anchor several corners of the park and offer strollers points of orientation (figure 104). A combination of hardy trees, shrubs, and berms define areas within the park. Royston does not wall off completely the various spaces with vegetation but allows park users to catch glimpses into adjacent precincts to draw them deeper into the park. The view from inside the chain tent exemplifies this masterful orchestration of views. From inside the structure the eye is drawn out beneath the canopy (*Wisteria chinensis*) through windows created by support columns and small trees (*Pittosporum tobira*) that ring the space (figure 105). The view continues past turf-covered berms, some tall enough to direct sightlines toward the lake and its large fountain jet. Majestic coast red-

103. CENTRAL PARK, SANTA CLARA, 1960–75. THE MASSIVE, HOLLOWED-OUT GRANITE CUBES FORMING PART OF THE PARK'S MOST ELABORATE PLAY STRUCTURE. [RHAA]

104. CENTRAL PARK. A TYPICAL REDWOOD GROVE BORDERING ON ONE OF THE LARGE LAWN SPACES. [REUBEN RAINEY, 2005]

105. CENTRAL PARK. LOOKING THROUGH THE WISTERIA WINDOWS OF THE PICNIC PAVILION. [REUBEN RAINEY, 2006]

woods (*Sequoia sempervirens*) and bigleaf maples (*Acer macrophylla*) form a distant backdrop that encloses and terminates the composition.

As at Mitchell Park, the perimeters are not buffered in order to open views into the interior. The two large meadow spaces are left completely open, in contrast to the crisp layering of similar spaces with overlapping walls of trees at Mitchell Park and the Rod and Gun Club. Their undulating edges of deciduous and evergreen trees bear a family resemblance to Olmsted and Vaux's multi-use "greenswards" at Central and Prospect Parks and serve a similar function.[159] A day of South Bay sunshine attracts a multitude of sunbathers, Frisbee players, martial arts enthusiasts, and kite flyers.

Near the large picnic area west of Saratoga Creek, Royston and his colleagues built an earthen mound to showcase California's native vegetation. The plants were eventually obliterated by children who could not resist romping on the mound.[160] Today it is completely devoid of vegetation but remains popular as a play sculpture that invites headlong dashes down its slopes.

During later phases of the park's fifteen-year construction period, in the western portion

of the park Royston and his design team sited a community center (designed by architect George Matsumoto) with facilities for elderly citizens and a playground for retarded children. Both the eastern and western areas contain small spaces for concerts and dramatic performances, which Royston, with his interest in the performing arts, regarded as essential. The activities scheduled for the park's official dedication in 1974 proclaimed its many uses: music, a synchronized swimming and diving exhibition, sack races, a tennis exhibition, a water balloon toss, a tug of war, watermelon eating, a belly-dance exhibition, a baseball doubleheader, story time, a martial arts exhibition, and a safe boating demonstration.[161] Both in scale and sophistication Central Park is without question Royston's masterwork, drawing upon all that had preceded it and venturing into new formal explorations as well. It eventually gained both regional and national recognition. It was an important factor in the city of Santa Clara's receiving a 1966 National Gold Medal Award from the Chicago-based Sports Foundation, Inc., for its citywide recreation facilities.[162]

SANTA CLARA CIVIC CENTER PARK, 1964

Santa Clara Civic Center Park was another of Royston's collaborative efforts with Earl Carmichael and represented fresh design exploration in form and symbolic expression (figure 106). It forms the entry to the new twenty-three-acre civic center—opened in 1964 at a cost of almost two million dollars—that included the city hall, a municipal courts building, and the police administration building. The small three-acre park is located adjacent to the busy arterial El Camino Real, the original eighteenth-century Spanish colonial highway linking towns, forts, and missions in California. The vacant site had been intended for a new gas station but was purchased by the city just before construction began. Adjacent to a busy automotive strip and flanked by a four-lane entryway to the civic center, the small park is not very accessible to pedestrians but has ample parking on its north side. Like the shopping centers along El Camino Real, it is a drive-in facility.

The park takes the form of an asymmetrical water parterre. Its ground plane is defined by two rectangular pools joined by a narrow strip of water spanned by a small concrete bridge of layered slabs. The broad surfaces of the pools lend an air of serenity, and their graceful, curving raised edges create an ani-

106. SANTA CLARA CIVIC CENTER PARK, SANTA CLARA, 1964. SWEEPING CURVES AND A LOW-SLUNG TERRACE STAIR ARE TWO OF THE SUBTLE DETAILS THAT CONTRIBUTE TO THE FORMAL BEAUTY OF THE DESIGN. [RHAA]

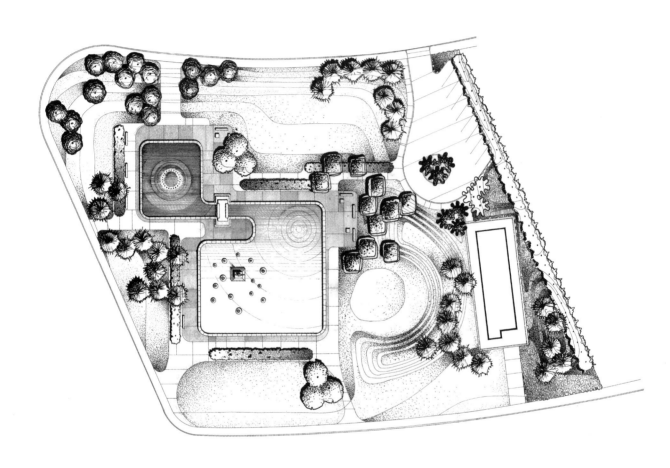

107. SANTA CLARA CIVIC CENTER PARK, SANTA CLARA, 1964. SITE PLAN. AN ASYMMETRICAL WATER PARTERRE DEFINES THE PARK'S CENTER. [EDA, UCB]

108. *(OPPOSITE PAGE)* SANTA CLARA CIVIC CENTER PARK. THE 3-ACRE PARK FORMS A GATEWAY TO THE CITY'S CIVIC CENTER. A GROUP OF NEWLY PLANTED OLIVE TREES BEHIND THE STATUE OF ST. CLARE SYMBOLIZES THE CITY'S HISTORY AS AN AGRICULTURAL CENTER. [MORLEY BAER, RHAA]

mated line that draws the eye around the perimeter (figure 107). A small spray fountain aerates the smaller pool to the north, adding soothing sound. The focal point of the entire composition is in the larger pool—a twenty-foot-high bronze, angular statue of Saint Clare by Anne Van Kleeck hovering over the water on a raised pedestal.[163] Dressed in her nun's habit, the city of Santa Clara's namesake is as serene as the water around her. The statue is placed off center, creating spatial tension in an otherwise harmonious composition. Fourteen circular planters with colorful flowers surround the statue and are elevated just a few inches above the water, creating the illusion they are floating on its surface (see figure 106). The pools are about a foot deep, a safety feature that also facilitates maintenance. A multiple jet fountain in the far corner of the pool gently animates its surface and forms a vertical counterpoint to the statue. To the east of the pool a lawn encircled by wisteria can serve as a small theatre, a signature element in Royston's designs by this time. The park also provides a convenient location for the city's small chamber of commerce building, which is located on its eastern edge.

Durable rectilinear concrete pavers define the ground plane around the pools and the major entry walks and contrast with the curvilinear lines of the pools (figure 108). With advice from his colleagues, Royston planted bosques of Mediterranean stone pines (*Pinus pinea*), maidenhair trees (*Ginkgo biloba*), and American sweetgum (*Liquidambar styraciflua*) throughout the site to shade the many custom-designed benches. Linear flowerbeds near the pool add accents of color and recall in form and placement Royston's work at Bowden Park nearly a decade earlier. Here they are more sophisticated, however, creating a slender, linear, color motif that complements the colors of the "floating" planters and contrasts with the park's predominantly green color palette. Also, Royston introduces a new element in his planting design, namely a touch of symbolism: Clusters of olive trees at each end of the site recall the expansive olive groves that once covered the South Bay and were a mainstay of Santa Clara's economy.

This small landscape serves more as an icon than a frequently used public park. Saint Clare's statue is easily visible to motorists speeding by on El Camino Real or cruising the four-lane access road to the civic center, perhaps reminding them of the Spanish roots of their city's history. It certainly functions as a vivid announcement of the main entry to the city's civic precinct. Since the park itself is a bit of a traffic island and is not bordered by restaurants

or other facilities that attract pedestrians, it tends to be little used on a day-to-day basis except by older citizens who in the hot summer months enjoy the shade of its bosks and the coolness of its evaporating pools. The lack of a playground limits its use by children. In terms of form, however, it is one of Royston's most elegant and serene designs.

After the Santa Clara Civic Center project, Royston continued to work with various design teams in his professional office on other park commissions. The basic concept of parks as public gardens, where form and function in concert engage the senses, remained the guiding principle of many later designs. By the year 1990, when Royston retired from full-time practice, the firm's park projects had grown to include nine national and state parks, ten regional and county parks, and 109 city and community parks, including projects in Singapore and Malaysia.[164] While the scope of this work tended to be quite large, its basic conceptual ideas and individual design elements were to a great degree a creative rephrasing of Royston's innovative work of the 1950s.

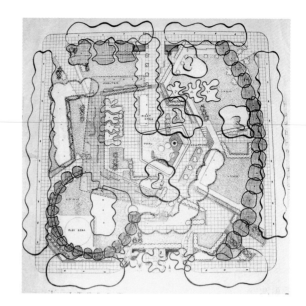

109. CITY PLAZA PARK, SACRAMENTO, 1947. NOT ALL OF ROYSTON'S POSTWAR PARK DESIGNS WERE INTENDED FOR THE SUBURBS. THIS EARLY DESIGN FOR A ROOFTOP PARK OVER A GARAGE WAS NOT CONSTRUCTED. THE BIOCUBIC FORMS ARE SIMILAR TO THOSE DEVELOPED IN THE MITCHELL PARK PLAYGROUND A DECADE LATER. [EDA, UCB]

110. ST. MARY'S SQUARE PARK, SAN FRANCISCO, 1957. ANOTHER OF ROYSTON'S PARK DESIGNS ATOP A PARKING GARAGE IN A DENSELY POPULATED URBAN SETTING. THE LARGE AREAS OF PAVING ALLOW FOR HIGH VOLUMES OF FOOT TRAFFIC. [EDA, UCB]

111. (OPPOSITE PAGE) ST. MARY'S SQUARE PARK. THE LONG BENCHES AND GRACEFULLY CURVING SEAT WALLS ACCOMMODATE LARGE CROWDS SEEKING RESPITE FROM THE HECTIC PACE OF THE CITY. [RHAA]

CONCLUSION:
A REPERTORY OF PUBLIC GARDENS

When Royston characterized his suburban parks as public gardens, that concept was subtle and multifaceted. These seven examples designed by Royston in the first twenty years of his professional practice, with some advice from his partners, reveal the extensive repertory of scale, function, type, and design vocabulary typical of his early park work. There is a sturdy consistency to that repertory: the biocubic forms carefully scaled to human activity, the play areas that engage a child's imagination and offer physical challenges, the enlarged residential garden details, the sophisticated use of plants and berms to define spaces, the marking of the seasons with planted form, the carefully orchestrated promenades for discovery and multisensual experience, the provision for civic ritual and group events, and the range of facilities to delight people of all ages. The smaller-scale, more specialized Santa Clara Civic Center Park lacks the full range of the repertory, but its family resemblance to Royston's other public spaces is unmistakable.

Over these two decades Royston's repertory does exhibit changes, which are confined mostly to design details. More rustic log structures and stone walls appear at Bowden and Central Parks, adding greater variety of materials that emphasize texture. Central Park's more naturalistic edge treatments in the large lawn spaces contrast with Mitchell Park's more geometrical tree walls. An experiment with Mondrian-like geometry at Bowden Park introduces a fresh design idiom. The large picnic tent and pergola at Central Park venture into civic monumentality. Otherwise, Royston's design method, spatial articulation, and use of forms remain mostly constant. This is hardly a matter of design timidity. Royston witnessed the ongoing public enthusiasm for his early work at the Rod and Gun Club and Krusi Park and saw no need to tamper with success or to develop a newer vocabulary merely for its own sake. Indeed, his park designs for more densely populated cities, such as St. Mary's Square Park in San Francisco and City Plaza Park in Sacramento, closely resemble in form and detailing his suburban parks (figures 109, 110, 111).

The question now arises, how have these parks, some of which were built half a century ago, fared over time? The demographics of the Bay Area, as we noted in our analysis of Bowden Park, have changed radically. How have Royston's more recent parks adapted to this change? And have his older parks proved resilient and adaptable to the present multicultural environment with its kaleidoscopic lifestyles?

CHAPTER SEVEN

Continuity and Change: Park Designs after 1965

Royston continued to design parks for over thirty-five years. About ninety percent of the commissions were in California, and these eventually included 27 city and community parks on the San Francisco peninsula alone. Santa Clara commissioned the largest number of designs, with eight city and community parks.[165] Mirroring the trends of the 1970s and 1980s seen in the larger corporate landscape architecture offices, Royston's firm extended the scope of its practice both nationally and internationally to include park projects in the western United States, Canada, Asia, and South America.

The complexities of politics, economics, and the pre-existing urban patterns in the Bay Area had prevented Royston from designing a complete landscape matrix for any of the various municipalities that commissioned his work. However, the conditions offered by a recreation community in Oregon and a new town in Washington—nearly tabula rasas— finally allowed him to design comprehensive matrices at a larger scale than the one he had attempted at Ladera in 1946 at the beginning of his career. His designs for both Sun River, Oregon, a 5,500-acre residential community (1969), and North Bonneville, Washington, a new town (1974), featured a hierarchy of linked parks and recreational facilities that

112. SUN RIVER COMMUNITY PLAN, SUN RIVER, OREGON, 1972. THE EXTENSIVE PARK, TRAIL, AND OPEN SPACE SYSTEM ACHIEVED AT SUN RIVER IS THE FULLEST REALIZATION OF ROYSTON'S THEORETICAL CONCEPT OF THE "LANDSCAPE MATRIX." [RHAA]

113. CUESTA PARK, MOUNTAIN VIEW, 1974. THE SUBTLE SCULPTING OF THE GROUND PLANE IS SIMILAR TO MITCHELL AND CENTRAL PARKS. [MARC TREIB, 2004]

114. (OPPOSITE PAGE) RENGSTORFF PARK, MOUNTAIN VIEW, 1975. STONE AMPHITHEATER AND PICNIC AREA. [REUBEN RAINEY, 2004]

formed the sites' skeletal structures (figure 112). To his great satisfaction, both projects were constructed according to their original plans.[166]

These later team-designed landscapes bear a close family resemblance to the parks created by Royston in his first twenty years of practice (figure 113).[167] The greatest change was in play equipment. Mandatory safety standards and fears of litigation have required less risky and adventurous apparatuses. Custom design has given way to catalog equipment, steel to plastic.[168] In addition, concerns about vandalism have negated the use of the popular pedal-car freeways and giant checkerboards where the pieces were simply left in place overnight. Certain activities, such as shuffleboard and horseshoes, are no longer popular and have been removed. Skate board ramps have been added to a few of the new parks. Yet much remains. Swimming pools, playfields, multi-use community centers, theaters, barbecue areas, and picnic grounds continue to please a much more ethnically diverse population than the predominantly Anglo audience of the 1950s.[169] In particular, the great sweeps of lawn in these newer parks can adapt to both time-honored pursuits and the latest recreational crazes. The touch football contest unfolds next to the pick-up soccer game,

and a bit farther on, the landscape painting class quietly works next to the storytelling group, which in turn is located near the obedience session at the bermed-off dog run. Some of these later California parks noteworthy for both design sophistication and popularity are Cuesta Park and Rengstorff Park, Mountain View; Las Positas Park, Santa Barbara; Bowers Park and Homestead Park, Santa Clara; and Millbrae Park, Millbrae (figure 114).[170]

THE PRESENT STATE OF THE EARLIER PARKS

If we use a human analogy, several of Royston's earlier parks are approaching their mid-fifties, having left behind the bloom of youth and full adulthood and now approaching the threshold of their senior-citizen years. How have they fared over time? Their fate is, of course, inextricably tied to the economic health of their communities. The parks on the San Francisco peninsula, nourished by the large tax coffers of Silicon Valley municipalities, have for the most part flourished even though in some cases maintenance budgets have been reduced during economic recessions. This is especially true of the Palo Alto parks. In Alameda in the East Bay the story is different. At Krusi Park

all of the original play equipment has been removed, the victim of slashed city budgets, litigation fears, and vandalism. Where schoolchildren once cruised the figure-eight freeway in their pedal-cars, all that remains is turf and a few inexpensive swings and slides.

Some parks have suffered decline but have been restored. Some have continued to flourish with little change. Mitchell Park is an example of the former; Santa Clara's Central Park and the Rod and Gun Club, the latter.

During the decades of the 1970s and 1980s Mitchell Park suffered a slow decline due to poor maintenance and vandalism, a deadly combination that has destined many a city park to near oblivion. For reasons of security, Palo Alto's department of parks and recreation removed the redwood screens that defined the picnic areas and senior citizens' recreation facilities. The pedal-car freeway and A-frame garages were disassembled because the local fire department no longer had the time to maintain the cars. Much of the original play equipment was considered unsafe and removed. The adjacent schools continued to use the play-fields, but during the 1980s the park deteriorated for lack of sufficient maintenance funds. The one positive note was the maturing of the vegetation. Large stone pines formed spatial

umbrellas on the lawn areas, and the redwood groves at the corners of the park had grown tall and created shade for picnickers. Also, the trunks of the sycamores surrounding the multi-use circular slab created a striking colonnade.

In the 1990s the Palo Alto department of parks and recreation decided to transform the deteriorated park. The city's tax base had benefited from the growing prosperity of Silicon Valley, of which Stanford University and the city itself were an integral part. Thus funds were available for renewal of the park as well as of the entire Palo Alto park system.

This time citizen input was a decisive factor in determining the fate of Mitchell Park. Palo Alto citizens tend to be highly educated, prosperous, strongly opinionated, and active in civic affairs; many are second- and third-generation residents, an exception to the mobility of many Bay Area suburbanites. Thus, a considerable number of adults held vivid memories of the park from their child-hood days. A spirited debate emerged at city council meetings. One group wanted a complete redesign of the park with safe, state-of-the-art play equipment. Another called for restoring the park to its 1950s condition, noting the historical significance of the design as well as their fond personal memories of the delightful place it had been before decline set in. This group was joined by children in the nearby schools who stood before the city council and pleaded for a restoration that would bring back much of its play equipment, which they knew only in its dilapidated shape.[171]

In the end the two sides were able to meld their visions, and the department of parks and recreation agreed. It was a wise solution that recognized a design does not have to be fifty years old to merit preservation. The city commissioned the Berkeley landscape architectural firm of Dillingham Associates to produce a plan and working drawings that restored many of the original 1958 features and adapted others to twenty-first-century conditions. Royston himself, now retired, served as a consultant, and some modifications were made to the original plan. The graceful, curving redwood fences were not reinstated for reasons of security. This was a considerable loss visually, but the original plants alongside the fences had matured, giving strong spatial definition to the park's zones. The new plan retained little of the original play equipment, which was judged unsafe, but the graceful biocubic forms of the young children's play areas have been redesigned to suit new equipment and respond to the current codes and safety guidelines.[172] The whimsical concrete bear

sculptures that had delighted children for two generations were cleaned and restored (figure 115). The children's wading pool fell victim to safety and maintenance concerns and was replaced by a spray pad with no depth (figure 116). The ever-popular gopher holes were left untouched because recreating them in conformance with current construction standards was not economically feasible and they were judged sufficiently safe (figure 117).

Welcome additions were the reading circle and kitchenette for birthday parties. A large dog run, separated from the rest of the park by a fence and screened visually by a large berm, replaced the parking area on the south side of the park. The small community building, with its offices and multipurpose room, was completely refurbished.

Most of the new construction was completed by 2003, and park maintenance has been much improved. The park and recreation department also approved a part-time recreation director who developed a diverse program of activities for all ages. On a typical weekend one can observe everything from storytelling, art classes in plein air, Tai Chi, and chess games to a full program of organized team sports that include baseball, soccer, and roller blade hockey. The park is also the venue for all-city events such as a chili cookoff. There is some-

thing for all age groups, and the park is one of the most used in Palo Alto, attracting individuals from many surrounding municipalities. Ironically, a site that was derelict and little used is now threatened by overuse.[173]

In Point Richmond, to the north, the Rod and Gun Club is mostly intact and heavily used on weekends. Regular maintenance has allowed this early park to achieve a lifespan of nearly fifty years. While much of the more adventuresome play equipment has been removed, a representative sample of the original equipment remains in good condition for its age although perhaps in need of a new coat of paint (figure 118). The timid heights and prominent safety railings on the new post-and-platform play structures create a noticeable—almost ironic—contrast with their more dramatic and robust forebears (see figure 61). Sadly, the elegant, curving wooden fences that functioned as windbreaks in the sunbathing area were removed when their structural supports deteriorated, and they have not been replaced. Since the park is on private land in an oil refinery with limited access, the absence of fences is not a matter of security but of maintenance budgets. Almost five decades of shoreline plant growth has created an effective barrier to winds coming off the nearby bay, so the loss of the windscreens is primarily an aesthetic concern.[174]

Central Park in Santa Clara has flourished since its completion in the 1970s and has not required the surgery needed to resuscitate Mitchell Park. So successful was the original program that the parks and recreation department has resisted cluttering the park with new elements, choosing instead to carefully maintain or upgrade existing facilities. One addition has been a relatively small veterans' memorial tucked into the western perimeter of the park.

Larry Wolfe, who served as director of parks and recreation during the 1980s, referred to Central Park as the "heart of Santa Clara." Its International Swim Center has produced several Olympic champions and is a focus of civic pride. Santa Clarans frequently refer to their city as the "Swim Capital of the World."[175] This is chamber-of-commerce rhetoric to be sure, but the thousands of spectators who fill its bleachers month after month lend credence to it. The park is a venue for many civic events, including the Art and Wine Festival, which annually attracts up to 20,000 people. The two large-group picnic areas are booked six months in advance, and the large chain-and-wisteria pavilion has become a logo for various city publications. Softball and baseball associations, lawn bowling clubs, swim clubs, and tennis players make extensive use

115. *(OPPOSITE PAGE ABOVE)* MITCHELL PARK, PALO ALTO, 1956. THIS YOUNG SCULPTOR IS APPARENTLY CHANGING THE BEAR INTO A RHINOCEROS. [REUBEN RAINEY, 2005]

116. *(OPPOSITE PAGE MIDDLE)* MITCHELL PARK. THE NEW SPRAY PAD DESIGNED BY DILLINGHAM ASSOCIATES REPLACED THE ORIGINAL WADING POOL, BUT MAINTAINS ITS SHAPE. [REUBEN RAINEY, 2005]

117. *(OPPOSITE PAGE BELOW)* MITCHELL PARK. THE GOPHER HOLES CONTINUE TO DELIGHT. [REUBEN RAINEY, 2005]

118. STANDARD OIL ROD AND GUN CLUB, RICHMOND, 1950. TWO OF THE ORIGINAL SWINGS NOW SERVE THE WORKERS OF THE RENAMED CHEVRON REFINERY. [REUBEN RAINEY, 2003]

119. BOWDEN PARK, PALO ALTO, 1960. THE TREES HAVE MATURED, CREATING A DENSE CANOPY OVER THE SEATING AREAS. [REUBEN RAINEY, 2005]

of the park, as do patients and staff of a nearby hospital and children of the adjacent school. Real estate values for residences near the park are higher. In brief, Central Park has become a valued institution and, thanks to the high tax revenues, has been maintained in excellent condition. On a recent visit to the park, Royston, without identifying himself, asked a strolling couple what they thought of the park. The wife quipped, "I would not have married him unless he had promised to live near this park."[176] Questions to other users of all age groups elicited less hyperbole but comparable enthusiasm. On-site visits to Bowden Park, the Rod and Gun Club, and many other of Royston's Bay Area parks reveal similar enthusiasm among users (figure 119). Santa Clara's Civic Center Park continues to serve as an iconic entry to the civic center and is maintained in immaculate condition. Except for the maturity of its trees it is the most unchanged of all of Royston's park designs (figure 120).

120. SANTA CLARA CIVIC CENTER PARK, SANTA CLARA, 1964. EXCEPT FOR THE MATURING OF THE TREES, THIS PARK HAS REMAINED BASICALLY UNCHANGED FOR OVER FOUR DECADES. [REUBEN RAINEY, 2004]

CONCLUSION

In 1974 Robert Royston boarded a helicopter and cruised over the Bay Area at 800 feet, viewing his firm's projects and the general development pattern of the entire landscape. His first impression was deeply sobering, if not horrific:

We feel a sense of wonder at the evidence spread out below…How can so many solutions of the past cause so many problems for us today…the first and overpowering impression…is that the damage is irreparable; man's ability to wreck…and destroy is overwhelming.[177]

He looked for the work of his firm and others and found it buried in a "matrix of asphalt and sporadic zoning development"—polluted streams, vanished agricultural land, paved-over waterways, giant industrial complexes destroying small-scale neighborhoods, shoddy subdivision design, freeways that split formerly cohesive communities. The scroll of lost opportunities and callous error rolled on and on.[178]

Royston could have been describing just about any American city of the time, a familiar litany of haphazard growth and environmental degradation. However, he avoided a simplistic sermon about humanity as a cancer on the landscape, its propensity for greed, and the evils of capitalism—rants often delivered by some of his peers. Where it was all too easy to

see only mindless destruction and the abject failure of his hopes for a humane environment, hopes that had fueled his early career, Royston looked again and made a sober and modest assessment of what his firm and others had accomplished and pointed the way for future responses. He offered no utopian visions for the future but a few suggestions grounded in thirty years of experience in the rough coliseum of professional practice.

Royston saw islands of achievement in the sea of mistakes and lost opportunities, designs that brought meaning, sustenance, and delight into the lives of Bay Area citizens: Quiet pedestrian precincts of small college campuses, well-planned suburban developments, community and regional parks serving the recreational needs of a wide spectrum of age groups, bike paths and pedestrian trails connecting parks and communities, urban plazas and civic centers providing venues for civic rituals, clusters of residential gardens, and rooftop gardens on apartment buildings. These spaces may have been more noticeable by their scarcity, but they existed and they made a difference in people's lives. They also established precedents that could be built upon.[179]

Royston called for a reassertion of the idea of the landscape matrix and prophesied that the citizens of the Bay Area and other cities would demand it. He exhorted landscape architects to take the lead in promoting it and to commit their firms to the design of larger urban infrastructures. He also called for the rehabilitation of derelict areas savaged by industrial development and for the preservation of endangered ecosystems. The leitmotif of his optimism of the 1950s sounded clear, but more subtle and tempered, having matured in the ensuing years of professional encounters in the public realm.[180]

While Royston did not trumpet his own achievements, he could have taken pride in the more than sixty Bay Area parks he and his partners had designed, many of which, in 1974, were alive with the joy of sport, the restorative potency of nature, and the binding power of civic ritual.

Another thirty years has passed since Royston's helicopter ride. What of the present? The perennial and deceptively simple question "What is a park?" continues to challenge designers as it always will if their imaginations have not fossilized. The landscape matrix remains elusive; the two landscape architects who came closest about a century ago were Frederick Law Olmsted in his design for Boston's Emerald Necklace and Horace S. Cleveland, in the greater Minneapolis park system.[180] In the Bay Area the pieces are there,

but Royston's hope that citizens will demand their connection has yet to materialize.

In the past thirty years numerous original and engaging park designs have appeared in the work of Lawrence Halprin, Richard Haag, Peter Walker, Laurie Olin, Michael Van Valkenburg, Martha Schwartz, Diana Balmori, Adriaan Geuze, Carol Johnson, Peter and Anneliese Latz, Warren Byrd, Mario Schjetnan, James Corner, Bernard Lassus, George Hargreaves, Ken Smith, Walter Hood, Julie Bargmann, Grant Jones, and others. Professionals and academics are beginning to produce a sophisticated and relevant body of park design theory.[182] Recent parks, both built and envisioned, manifest a number of new approaches; some embody a palimpsest of historical memory to instruct their users about the major events—both geological and historical—that have shaped their regions. Often this history features the former industrial use of the site. Still others call attention to and celebrate the natural processes of their surroundings with earthforms, vegetation, and individual pieces of sculpture that interact with the wind, tides, and seasonal change. Still others perform useful work such as flood control and wetlands preservation. Some emphasize the restorative power of immersion in a verdant

121. CENTRAL PARK, SANTA CLARA, 1960–75. WALLS OF FOLIAGE CLEARLY DEFINE THE SERENE CENTRAL LAKE AREA. [REUBEN RAINEY, 2005]

landscape with new vocabularies of planting design that go beyond the pastoral, picturesque, and sublime categories of the eighteenth and nineteenth centuries. Few of these parks are located on pristine agricultural land on the edges of suburbs like Royston's early parks. They are more likely to occupy derelict waterfronts and industrial sites where dangerous pollutants require high-tech intervention to render them safe for human beings.[183]

Royston's parks have much to offer in this ongoing debate and exploration of the nature and function of parks. Far from being quaint survivors of an earlier age, their continuing use in relatively unaltered form and enthusiastic support by the citizens and government officials in several municipalities attest to their design excellence. They deserve to be a part of today's discussion of park design given their proven strengths in several areas. Royston's vision of the landscape matrix is difficult to achieve given the sobering realities of politics and real estate economics, but even an approximation of it is a boon to a city. An integrated system of nature preserves and recreation areas that connect a city's civic, educational, and residential areas is a sturdy skeleton that supports and enlivens the urban body. Parks that are readily accessible to citizens of all ages, allowing them a wide range of

recreational choices from solitary musing to exhilarating team sports, are an integral part of this matrix. In addition, as in Royston's parks, there should be opportunities for civic rituals, educational activities, and a chance to encounter the restorative power of lushly planted spaces. Style is not the issue. One may or may not embrace the beauty of line and stimulating complexities of Royston's biocubic forms. What is essential, as Royston so aptly understands, is, whatever the form, it must be carefully calibrated to human use—not art for art's sake, but art for humanity's sake. Human needs and the protection of the natural environment are the proper catalysts of form. In addition, as in Royston's parks, various activities should be carefully zoned to avoid conflict. Such zoning is best achieved not by the simple placement of objects but by creating spaces scaled to the activities they frame (figure 121).

If we were to repeat Royston's helicopter ride today over the Bay Area, we would observe that the "synopolis" or "galactic city" has grown even larger and continues to manifest all of the problems that generated Royston's sober assessment of thirty years ago. Yet as we circle low over the San Francisco peninsula and look carefully between the Coastal Range and the Bay at Mountain View, Woodside, Palo Alto, Hillsborough, and Santa Clara, green polygon after green polygon will appear like patches woven into the gray crazy quilt of office parks, warehouses, shopping centers, and tract houses. Some border stream valleys; most are adjacent to schools and libraries. They vary in size from a few acres to about fifty. Many but not all of them are the work of Royston and his partners, and if we are permitted to land in the midst of one of them on a weekend, we will find them filled with individuals engaged in the grace of sport, the joy of play, and the bonding power of civic events. These parks engage us with their imaginative response to human needs, their elegant form, and their total lack of pretension. Here are no iconographic programs or arcane references to regional history to be decoded. They are spaces that have stood the test of time in one of the most ephemeral of all arts, landscape architecture. They challenge us to do as well or better as we continue to struggle to bring order and amenity to the ever-expanding twenty-first-century city, a city of increasing ethnicity and multiple living arrangements in which the traditional nuclear family is in the minority, a city with great polarities of wealth and poverty and ever-growing threats to the ecosystems that sustain the health and welfare of its citizens.

Notes

1 See, for example, the simplistic analysis of John Keats, *The Crack in the Picture Window* (Boston: 1956), and Richard E. Gordon et al., *The Split-Level Trap* (New York, 1962).

2 Conversation with Robert N. Royston, 14 March 2002.

3 Conversation with Royston, 26 January 2003.

4 Ibid.

5 Quoted in Michael Laurie, with David Streatfield, *75 Years of Landscape Architecture at Berkeley, An Informal History, Part I: The First 50 Years* (Berkeley: Department of Landscape Architecture, University of California Berkeley, 1988), 31.

6 Laurie, 22-25.

7 Conversation with Royston, 26 January 2003.

8 Laurie, 24.

9 Ibid., 27-28.

10 Ibid., 28.

11 Quoted in Laurie, 28.

12 Ibid.

13 Conversation with Royston, 26 January 2003.

14 See Garrett Eckbo, Daniel U. Kiley, and James C. Rose, "Landscape Design in the Primeval Environment," *Architectural Record*, vol. 87, no. 2 (February 1940): 74-79; "Landscape Design in the Rural Environment," *Architectural Record*, vol. 86, no. 8 (August 1939): 68-74; "Landscape Design in the Urban Environment," *Architectural Record*, vol. 85, no. 5 (May 1939): 70-77.

15 See *Contemporary Landscape Architecture* (San Francisco: San Francisco Museum of Art, 1937), 15-19, 21-25.

16 Conversation with Royston, 18 January 2003.

17 Quoted in Laurie, 31.

18 Conversation with Royston, 28 January 2003.

19 Conversation with Royston, 14 March 2002.

20 John J. Wallace, "Robert Royston Landscape Architect." Master's thesis, Graduate Division, University of California, Berkeley, 1992, 7-12.

21 Quoted in Wallace, 7.

22 Quoted in Wallace, 14.

23 Conversation with Royston, 28 January 2003.

24 Ibid.

25 Conversation with Royston, 14 March 2002.

26 Ibid.

27 Mel Scott, *The San Francisco Bay Area: A Metropolis in Perspective*, 2nd ed. (Berkeley: University of California Press, 1985), 271.

28 Ibid., 250-51.

29 See Kevin Starr, *Inventing the Dream, California Through the Progressive Era* (New York and Oxford: Oxford University Press, 1985), chaps. 2, 5, 6, 9, & 10.

30 Scott, 275, 280-84.

31 James E. Vance, Jr., *Geography and Urban Evolution in the San Francisco Bay Area* (Berkeley: Institute of Governmental Studies, 1964), 89.

32 Peirce F. Lewis, "The Unprecedented City," *The American Land* (New York: W. W. Norton and Company, 1979), 184-86.

33 Laurie, 37, 50-51.

34 For a representative example of work of the Bay Area landscape architects from the 1940s and 1950s, see the exhibition catalogs *Landscape Design* (San Francisco: San Francisco Museum of Art and Association of Landscape Architects, San Francisco Region, 1948) and *Landscape Architecture 1958*, R. Burton Litton Jr., ed. (San Francisco: San Francisco Museum of Art, 1958). For a brief account of the period, see Laurie, chaps. 4 & 5.

35 According to Royston, several of his designs from the period when he was heading the San Francisco office of Eckbo, Royston and Williams are illustrated in Garrett Eckbo's *Landscape for Living* (New York: F. N. Dodge Corporation, 1950). These are identified under the general heading Eckbo, Royston, and Williams and include "Twin Gardens in Marin County California, 1948" (142-43), which are the houses and gardens Royston and his friend the architect Joseph Stein built for themselves. According to Royston, other illustrations of his work are "Garden in Woodside Hills, California, 1947" (154-55), commissioned by the Naify family; "The Country Home in Marin County, 1946" (158-59); "The Ranch House in Central Valley of California," 1945 (158-59). The park designs in *Landscape for Living* are primarily Eckbo's work for the Farm Security Administration. None of the parks shown are by Royston. Conversation with Royston, 14 March 2002.

36 See the excellent essays on the career of Thomas Church in Marc Treib, ed., *Thomas Church Landscape Architect, Designing a Modern California Landscape* (San Francisco: William Stout Publishers, 2003).

37 Laurie, 45.

38 The most comprehensive treatment of the history of American parks is Galen Cranz, *The Politics of Park Design, A History of Urban Parks in America* (Cambridge, MA: MIT Press, 1982).

39 There are many excellent studies of Olmsted and Vaux's park work. Among the best are Cynthia Zaitzevsky, *Frederick Law Olmsted and the Boston Park System* (Cambridge, MA: The Belknap Press of Harvard University Press, 1982); David Schuyler, *The New Urban Landscape, The Redefinition of Urban Form in Nineteenth-Century America* (Baltimore: The Johns Hopkins University Press, 1986); Albert Fein, ed., *Landscape into Cityscape, Frederick Law Olmsted's Plans for a Greater New York City* (Ithaca, NY: Cornell University Press, 1967); Elizabeth Barlow Rogers, *Landscape Design, A Cultural and Architectural History* (New York: Harry N. Abrams, Inc., 2001); and Charles E. Beveridge and Paul Rocheleau, *Frederick Law Olmsted: Designing the American Landscape* (New York: Rizzoli, 1995).

40 Conversation with Royston, 10 July 2002.

41 Ibid.

42 Zaitzevsky, 54–58, 66–73, 81–93.

43 Cranz, 69, and Henry V. Hubbard, "Parks and Playgrounds, Their Requirements and Distribution as Elements in the City Plan," *Landscape Architecture*, vol. XII, no. 4 (July 1922): 242.

44 The following analysis of developments in urban park design from the late nineteenth century to the 1930s is heavily indebted to Cranz, 61–99. As Cranz points out, in much design parlance in the late nineteenth century the word *park* had become a vague generic designation applied to a wide variety of urban outdoor spaces. This blurring of the term occurred as park departments, paralleling the formation of fire departments and police departments, became part of the bureaucracy of municipal governments. Park administrations found themselves in charge of a wide variety of urban spaces, including playing fields, public gardens, monument sites, and leftover parcels of land at street intersections, all of which shared the name park.

45 See Playground and Recreation Association of America, *Play Areas: Their Design and Equipment*, (New York: A. S. Barnes and Company, 1928), and Cranz, 93–96.

46 Henry V. Hubbard, "The Size and Distribution of Playgrounds and Similar Recreation Facilities in American Cities," *Landscape Architecture*, vol. IV, no. 4 (July 1914): 133–44; and "Parks and Playgrounds, Their Requirements and Distribution as Elements in the City Plan," *Landscape Architecture*, vol. XII, no. 4 (July 1922): 240–64; Henry V. Hubbard and Theodora Kimball, *An Introduction to the Study of Landscape Design* (New York: The Macmillan Company, 1917), 295–98.

47 Hubbard, "The Size and Distribution of Playgrounds," 133–35.

48 Hubbard, "Parks and Playgrounds, Their Requirements," 244.

49 See L. H. Weir, ed., *Parks, A Manual of Municipal and County Parks* (New York: A.S. Barnes and Company, 1928); George D. Butler, *Recreation Areas, Their Design and Equipment* (New York: A. S. Barnes and Company, 1947); and the following articles on theories of park design from *Parks and Recreation*: W. Allen Perry, "Are Parks Here to Stay?," vol. 43, no. 3 (March 1960): 130 ff; Conrad L. Wirth, "Parks Are For People," vol. 42, no. 6 (June 1959): 202 ff.; William Penn Mott, Jr., "Changing Land Use Patterns," vol. 38 (May 1955): 1.

50 Weir, *Parks, A Manual*, 1–13.

51 In 1946, Weir wrote that the American people had developed "an entirely new conception of life." No longer did they believe, as did their ancestors, that life was a "purgatory" that "refines" the soul for an afterlife free from all earthly ills. They have discovered that "leisure had come to earth with all its promises of the human mind and soul…" They are "affirming a richer and happier life here," and "the quality of this life of leisure will be the new means of success rather than the old one based on the accumulation of material things." ("Historical Background of Recreation in America," *Parks and Recreation*, July-August 1946, 238-243). For all of its blissful naïveté, this prophecy expresses a somewhat extreme form of the can-do optimism of many planners and designers during the postwar economic recovery. Royston did not share Weir's naïve optimism.

52 Conversation with Royston, 10 July 2003.

53 Ibid.

54 See *Report on a General Plan for the City of Santa Clara, California* (Millbrae, CA, December 1959), 110. This report cites *Planning the Neighborhood* in its bibliography and advocates an approach to park design that agrees with most of its recommendations. *Report on the Interim General Plan, City of Palo Alto*, April 1955 (Palo Alto, CA: City Planning Commission, 1955) does not cite the study but sets forth policies on park design that are also very similar to it (see 73-79). The same is true for *A Master Plan for Palo Alto, Preliminary Draft*, 27 June, 1949, L. Deming Tilton, Planning Consultant (Palo Alto, CA), see chapter 8: 1-11.

55 Allan A. Twichell., ed, American Public Health Association Committee on the Hygiene of Housing, Public Administration Service, *Planning the Neighborhood*, (Chicago: R. R. Donneley and Sons, 1948), v-vii, 1-3.

56 Ibid., 1.

57 Ibid., 1-2.

58 Arthur B. Gallion and Simon Eisner, *The Urban Pattern, City Planning and Design* (New York: D. Van Nostrand Company, Inc., 1963), 250-54. Gallion and Eisner refer to N. L. Engelhardt, Jr., "The School Neighborhood Nucleus," *Architectural Forum*, 1943, and Clarence Perry, *The Neighborhood Unit*, Vol 7, *Neighborhood and Community Planning, Regional Survey, New York and Its Environs* (New York, 1929). This theory was influential well into the 1970s until school busing and consolidation made it no longer feasible for many communities throughout the country.

59 *Planning the Neighborhood*, 27.

60 Ibid., 47.

61 Ibid., 72.

62 Ibid., 47.

63 *Guide for Planning Recreation Parks in California, A Basis for Determining Local Recreation Space*, California Committee on Planning for Recreation, Park Areas and Facilities (Sacramento, CA: Printing Division Documents Section, 1956), 9-10. The committee included Bay Area landscape architect Theodore Osmundson, Jr. William Penn Mott, Jr., Superintendent of Parks, Oakland, was a consultant to the committee as well.

64 Ibid., 51, 53, 55, 61, 63, 64.

65 Ibid., 23.

66 This latter recommendation sounds a bit like a benign version of William Golding's *Lord of the Flies* or the latest pop psychology notion of the "primitive" nature of children's play.

67 *Guide for Planning Recreation Parks in California*, 48, 56-59. The *Guide* divided the state into six regions determined by population, "historical association," climate, settlement pattern, economic activity, vegetation, and topography and tailored its guidelines to each region. The specifications cited here apply to the "coastal metropolitan" region, which includes the San Francisco Bay area.

68 Conversation with Royston, 10 July 2003.

69 As quoted by Cranz, 122. See also Eckbo's article in the March 1948 issue of *Parks and Recreation*, 99-105. In this essay he accepts the neighborhood unit as the basis of the design of park systems and, like Royston, advocates a city of "continuous park patterns."

70 Conversation with Royston, 10 July 2003.

71 See Robert N. Royston: "Is There a Bay Area Style?" *Architectural Record* vol. 105 (May 1949), 96; "Standard's Employees Do It Themselves," *Landscape Architecture*, vol. 55, no. 1 (October 1964, Section One), 51ff; "Looking Down on the San Francisco Bay Area," *Landscape Architecture*, vol. 64, no. 4 (July 1974), 234-43; "Getting the Feel for a New Town Site and Its Design," *Landscape Architecture*, vol. 66, no. 5 (Spring 1976), 432-43; "Point of View," *Landscape Architecture*, vol. 76, no. 6 (November-December 1986), 66-67, 116; "A Brief History," *Landscape Australia*, vol. 8, no. 1 (Fall 1986), 34-36, 38; "Robert Royston's Thoughts on Landscape Architecture," *Landscape Australia*, vol. 8, no. 2 (Winter 1986), 152-64.

72 Robert Royston, "Mary Kim McKeown First Memorial Lecture Notes," 14 May 1992, unpublished manuscript in Royston's personal papers, 2.

73 Conversation with Royston, 14 March 2002.

74 Robert Royston, "On Foreign Work," August 1985, unpublished manuscript in Royston's personal papers, 1-2.

75 Royston, McKeown Lecture, 3.

76 Robert Royston, "Robert Royston's Thoughts on Landscape Architecture," *Landscape Australia*, vol. 8, no. 2 (Winter 1986): 154. Royston's position, while not developed in detail, is somewhat similar to those of Edward

O. Wilson and Jay Appleton. See
Edward O. Wilson, *Biophilia, The
Human Bond with Other Species*
(Cambridge, MA: Harvard University
Press, 1984), 103-18; and Jay Appleton,
The Experience of Landscape, rev. ed.
(West Sussex, England: John Wiley
and Sons Ltd., 1996). However, Wilson
and Appleton are discussing human
habitat preferences, not design princi-
ples per se.

77 Robert Royston, letter to Ervin H.
Zube, Professor of Landscape
Architecture, University of Arizona,
1990 (precise date lacking) Royston
personal papers.

78 Conversation with Royston, 11
March 2002.

79 Ibid.

80 Quoted in Wallace, 25.

81 Steven C. Pepper, "Introduction
to Garden Design," in San Francisco
Museum of Art, *Landscape Design*,
1948, 5.

82 Royston, "A Brief History," 38.

83 Conversation with Robert
Royston, 14 March 2002.

84 Marc Treib and Dorothée Imbert,
*Garrett Eckbo, Modern Landscapes
for Living* (Berkeley: University of
California Press, 1997), 59-67.

85 Conversation with Robert
Royston, 26 January 2003.

86 Royston, McKeown Lecture, 3.

87 Royston, "Robert Royston's Thoughts
on Landscape Architecture," 154.

88 Robert Royston, "Thoughts on
Landscape Architecture," 19 August,
1985, unpublished manuscript,
Royston's personal papers, 3.

89 Conversation with Royston, 10
July 2002.

90 Royston, "Robert Royston's
Thoughts on Landscape Architecture,"
153.

91 Royston, McKeown Lecture, 2.

92 John Dixon Hunt and Peter Willis,
*The Genius of the Place, The English
Landscape Garden 1620-1820*, eds.
(Cambridge, MA: The MIT Press, 1988),
37-38.

93 Transcript of recorded conversation
with Royston, 27 July 2003.

94 Conversation with Royston, 26
January 2003.

95 Royston, "Thoughts on Landscape
Architecture," 3.

96 Royston, "Robert Royston's
Thoughts on Landscape Architecture,"
152.

97 Conversation with Royston, 14
March 2002.

98 Royston, "Robert Royston's Thoughts
on Landscape Architecture," 154.

99 Royston, "A Brief History," 38.

100 *The American Heritage Dictionary
of the English Language*, ed. William
Morris (Boston: Houghton Mifflin Co.,
1981), 543.

101 See Phoebe Cutler, *The Public
Landscape of the New Deal* (New
Haven, CT: Yale University Press,
1985), 43-44.

102 See the examples of Royston's
work included in Garrett Eckbo's
Landscape for Living, 142-43, 154-55,
158-59.

103 For numerous examples, see
Cutler, *The Public Landscape of the
New Deal*, 39-45. See also L. H. Weir,
*Parks, A Manual of Municipal and
County Parks*, vol. 1, and George D.
Butler, *Recreation Areas, Their Design
and Equipment*.

104 Cutler, 41-42.

105 Conversation with Royston, 8
August 2003.

106 *Play Areas, Their Design and
Equipment*, 112. In the mid-1960s
Royston was commissioned to add
new playgrounds and a swimming
pool to Rinconada Park, altering it to
serve a wider range of age groups.

107 Weir, *Parks, A Manual*, 147, and
Play Areas, 121. In the early postwar
period designers in Europe and
England began to explore new design
vocabularies primarily for playgrounds
in an urban context. For an overview
of park and playground design in
Europe, England, and the United
States from 1945-1959, see Alfred
Ledermann and Alfred Trachsel,
*Creative Playgrounds and Recreation
Centers* (New York: Frederick A.
Praeger, 1959). Royston's Krusi Park,
Mitchell Park, and a park for Corte
Madera, California, are included in
this study. The 1968 revised edition of
this work is also a useful reference.

108 Conversation with Royston, 10
July 2002.

109 Ibid.

110 Conversation with Royston, 3
March 2003.

111 Conversation with Royston, 8
August 2003.

112 Ibid.

113 Conversation with Royston, 10
August 2003.

114 Ibid.

115 Conversation with Royston, 26 January 2003. See also Treib and Imbert, *Garrett Eckbo*, 48-55.

116 Treib and Imbert, 147–48.

117 Ibid., 150.

118 Ibid., 106-46.

119 Ibid., 129-43.

120 Sketches of these playgrounds as well as a plan for Ladera appeared in Eckbo's *Landscape for Living*, 222-23.

121 We are indebted to Leo Marx for the term "middle landscape." See his classic study, *The Machine in the Garden, Technology and the Pastoral Ideal in America* (Oxford: Oxford University Press, 1964).

122 R. Burton Litton Jr., ed., "Designing Parks for Children," *Parks and Recreation*, vol. 42, no. 6 (June 1959): 272 ff, and *Landscape Architecture 1958*, 11. Royston also published a brief description of the park, "Standard's Employees Do It Themselves," *Landscape Architecture*, vol. 55, no. 1 (October 1964): 51ff.

123 The bent tubular framework of the long, linear pergolas has proven to be extremely durable after over fifty years of continuous use.

124 The December 1957 issue of *Pacific Architect and Builder with Construction News Bulletin* featured the large slide on its cover. In the same issue a brief article, "For Employees: Relaxation in the Sun or the Shade," praised the park for its innovative design, 18-20.

125 *Guide for Planning Recreation Parks in California*, 48.

126 William Penn Mott, Jr., "Children's Fairyland," *Parks and Recreation*, vol. 42, no. 5 (March 1951): 5-7, and "Magic Key to Your Park's Story," *Parks and Recreation*, vol. 42, no. 5 (May 1959): 220 ff. Frank Caplan, president of Playsculptures, Inc., which built more sculptural abstract play apparatuses, in an article that was somewhat self-serving, also rejected the Fairyland approach for limiting a child's imagination. See Frank Caplan, "The Playgrounds of Tomorrow," *Parks and Recreation*, vol. 43, no. 1 (January 1960): 18 ff.

127 Conversation with Royston, 26 January 2003.

128 Ibid.

129 *Landscape Architecture 1958*, ed. R. Burton Litton, Jr, 23-24.

130 "Palo Alto's Mitchell Park, A West Coast Design Leader," *The American City*, vol. 72 (November 1957), 29; it was also included in *Landscape Architecture 1958*, ed. R. Burton Litton Jr., 11.

131 *Parks of Palo Alto* (Palo Alto: Palo Alto Historical Association, 1994), 48

132 Ibid., 48-51.

133 Conversation with Royston, 14 March 2002. Royston at times envisioned professional practice in terms of metaphors drawn from theatrical performance. A quote from him in a Royston Hanamoto Alley & Abey office brochure reads: "We know there is a growing audience for the gentle use of land and that we are on a stage to that audience . . . We project the image of what a landscape can be now and how it fits into the opportunities of the future. We should stay on stage, keep involved, improve capabilities and challenge the future always." Archives of Royston Hanamoto Alley & Abey, Mill Valley, CA (hereafter RHAA Archives).

134 Conversation with Royston, 14 March 2002.

135 Ibid.

136 A small photograph of the bears was included in *Landscape Architecture 1958*, 32.

137 Conversation with Royston, 14 March 2002.

138 Marc Treib has addressed this issue in relation to the work of Thomas Church: see Treib, "Mastery and Reflection," in *Thomas Church Landscape Architect*, 218-30.

139 *Guide for Planning Recreation Parks in California*, 48, 56-59.

140 Conversation with Royston, 15 November 2004.

141 *Guide for Planning Recreation Parks in California*, 59.

142 *Parks of Palo Alto*, 48.

143 Conversation with Royston, 9 July 2002.

144 Conversation with park users, predominantly young adults, male and female, 9 July 2002.

145 Conversation with Royston, 9 July 2002.

146 Photos taken shortly after the park's installation reveal that the city supplemented Royston's bold palette with additional annuals such as petunias and perennials with complementary foliage such as clumping blue fescue grass (*Festuca ovina* 'Glauca').

147 Conversation with Royston, 10 July 2002.

148 Ibid.

149 *Report on a General Plan for the City of Santa Clara, California*, 1959, 1-3, 18-22, 101-108.

150 Carmichael publicized the innovations and excellence of Santa Clara's park system in a number of national and state periodicals. See Earl R. Carmichael, "Park Plans Can Simplify Maintenance," *The American City*, October 1966, 104-6; "Make Your Parks People-Pleasers," *The American City*, April 1964, 104-6; and "Santa Clara Provides New Areas, Facilities Through Bond Issue," *California Park and Recreation Quarterly*, September 1963, 8-9.

151 Conversation with Royston, 10 July 2002.

152 Carmichael wrote in a letter to Elizabeth Muffeny, of the American Institute of Architects, recommending Royston for an Allied Professions Award: "He is one of the finest men that I have had the opportunity to work with and to know . . . I know him, not only as a very capable professional landscape architect, planner, environmentalist, but also, as a very wonderful, kind human being and a very close personal friend." Letter dated 24 July 1990, RHAA Archives.

153 Conversation with Royston, 10 July 2002.

154 Ibid.

155 Earl Carmichael, in a typically astute move, removed many of the trees on the site and replaced them with a golf driving range to raise additional money for the park while he lobbied city officials.

156 In the late 1980s the city of Santa Clara commissioned Royston's firm to make the picnic structure more accessible for the handicapped. A design team responded with new designs for the railings, ramps, and picnic furniture that would accommodate individuals in wheelchairs. Conversation with Royston, 10 July 1002.

157 Restroom and dishwashing facilities were also included in this area, and here Royston made the surprising suggestion that the roof of the restroom building should be planted with colorful flowers. The city went along with this then highly unusual idea and maintained an annual color garden on the roof of the small building for many years. Unfortunately, this quirky detail of the design eventually succumbed to the reality of the municipal maintenance routines and the building is now roofed in prosaic asphalt shingles.

158 This use of stronger textural detailing is a trend that continues in Royston's firm's park designs in the 1970s and 1980s.

159 This is another example of Royston's recognition that complex biocubic forms characteristic of his smaller park playgrounds cannot be read at a larger scale. After Central Park, Royston and his design teams tended to favor the open-center approach to these large turf areas. They recognized that the use of overlapping tree walls, while visually readable, tended to compartmentalize those spaces and restrict their flexibility of use. Conversation with Royston, 10 July 2002.

160 Ibid.

161 "All-City Picnic and Dedication of Central Park, Saturday, August 10, 1974," City of Santa Clara Parks and Recreation Department, 1974. RHAA Archives.

162 Also, in 1970 it received an Environmental Planning Award from the California Park and Recreation Society, and in 1974 it was selected for an Honor Award by the American Institute of Architects Miscellaneous uncataloged materials. RHAA Archives.

163 Saint Clare, the sister of St. Francis of Assisi, was the founder of an order of nuns. The statue cost $42,000. Some members of the Santa Clara Landmarks Commission at first favored another statue that was a more realistic depiction of St. Clare, but finally approved Van Kleeck's more abstract work. Robert Royston/RHAA Collection, Environmental Design Archives, University of California, Berkeley (hereafter EDA, UCB).

164 Robert Royston/RHAA Collection, "Parks and Re- creation," EDA, UCB. In a 1986 article Royston voiced strong support for working in design teams: "The age of the prima donna is long gone, because there are so many factors in every problem. It isn't just Bob Royston, it's Asa (Hanamoto), Kaz (Abey), Lou (Allen), Pat (Carlisle), Harold (Kobayashi) and members of the staff. I'm strong on the conceptual and very often behind the pencil, but others in the office are too. We're usually working in two or three person teams: it's a lot of fun and gets a better answer. You can't do it all alone." (Royston, "Point of View," *Landscape Architecture*, vol. 70 (November-December 1986: 13-14).

165 Robert Royston/RHAA Collection, "Parks and Recreation," EDA, UCB.

166 Conversation with Royston, 4 March 2003.

167 Typical examples are Cuesta Park and Rengstorff Park, Mountain View.

168 Today specialty companies design almost all play equipment used in parks. These firms often employ in-house teams of designers and social scientists specializing in the psychology of children's play. Also, such companies take full responsibility for any litigation involving their equipment. Typical examples are Playworld Systems, Inc., Miracle Recreation Equipment Company, Goric Marketing Group USA, Inc., and Park Structures, a PlayCore Company.

169 On-site observations of Bowden, Cuesta, Mitchell, Bowers, Westwood Oaks, Maywood, Bracher, Homestead, and Millbrae parks, 8 and 10 August 2003.

170 Cuesta Park received a prestigious Honor Award from the American Society of Landscape Architects in 1981.

171 Conversation with Royston, 14 March 2002.

172 Stephanie M. Peterson, a landscape architect with Dillingham Associates, has provided a succinct account of the redesign on the internet, "Revisiting Robert Royston's Mitchell Park": http://www.tclf.org/mitchell_park.htm.

173 Conversation with Royston, 8 August 2003.

174 On-site observations, 14 March 2002.

175 Miscellaneous uncataloged materials, RHAA Archives.

176 Conversation with Royston, 20 July 2002.

177 Robert Royston, "Looking Down on the San Francisco Bay Area," *Landscape Architecture*, vol. 64, no. 4 (July 1974): 234.

178 Ibid., 234.

179 Ibid., 236-39.

180 Ibid., 242.

181 Olmsted and Vaux's design for the Buffalo, NY, park system was also an important contribution.

182 The recent literature on the subject of park design is immense. A useful point of departure is Melanie Simo, *100 Years of Landscape Architecture: Some Patterns of a Century* (Washington, D.C.: ASLA Press, 1999), chaps. 5-7. Another source providing a broad perspective is Elizabeth Barlow Rogers, *Landscape Design*, chaps. 13-16. Articles in *Landscape Architecture* and *Landscape Journal* over the past decade deal with many issues involving park design. Also monographs on individual landscape architects published by Spacemaker Press, Washington, D.C., and the Japanese series, *Process Architecture* (Tokyo: Murotani Bunji Publisher) are other valuable resources.

183 Most recently Galen Cranz and Michael Boland have postulated the emergence in the late 1990s of "the sustainable park" in American, British, European, Australian, and Chinese landscape architectural design. According to them, three basic attributes characterize this park type: "(1) self-sufficiency in regard to material resources and maintenance, (2) solving larger urban problems outside of park boundaries, and (3) creating new standards for aesthetics and landscape management in parks and other urban landscapes." See Galen Cranz and Michael Boland, "Defining the Sustainable Park: A Fifth Model for Urban Parks," *Landscape Journal*, vol. 23, no. 2 (2004): 102-20.

Bibliography

Archives

Robert N. Royston / RHAA Collection, Environmental Design Archives, University of California, Berkeley.

Royston Hanamoto Alley & Abey Archives, Mill Valley, California.

Primary Sources

Royston, Robert N. "Is There a Bay Area Style?," *Architectural Record*, 105 (May 1949), 96.

———. "Standard's Employees Do It Themselves," *Landscape Architecture*, 55:1 (October 1964, Section One), 51 ff.

———. "Looking Down on the San Francisco Bay Area," *Landscape Architecture*, 64:4 (July 1974), 234-243.

———. "Getting the Feel for a New Town Site and Its Design," *Landscape Architecture*, 66:5 (Spring 1976), 432-443.

———. "On Foreign Work," August 1985. Unpublished manuscript in Royston's personal papers.

———. "Point of View," *Landscape Architecture*, 76:6 (November-December 1986), 66-67, 116.

———. "A Brief History," *Landscape Australia*, 8:1 (Fall 1986), 34-36, 38.

———. "Robert Royston's Thoughts on Landscape Architecture," *Landscape Australia*, 8:2 (Winter 1986), 152-164.

———. "Mary Kim McKeown First Memorial Lecture Notes," 14 May 1992. Unpublished manuscript in Royston's personal papers.

Secondary Sources

American Public Health Association Committee on Hygiene of Housing. *Planning the Neighborhood*. Chicago: R. R. Donnelley and Sons, 1948.

Appleton, Jay. *The Experience of Landscape*, rev. ed. West Sussex, England: John Wiley and Sons Ltd., 1996.

Beveridge, Charles E., and Paul Rocheleau. *Frederick Law Olmsted: Designing the American Landscape*. New York: Rizzoli, 1995.

Brockman, C. Frank. "Concepts of Recreation," *Recreation*, 52: 8 (October 1959), 309.

Burnap, George. *Parks, Their Design Equipment and Use*, Prepared for National Recreation Association. Philadelphia: J. B. Lippincott Company, 1916.

Butler, George D. "Our Space Standards," *Recreation*, 51:1 (January 1958), 24-26.

———. *Recreation Areas, Their Design and Equipment*. New York: A. S. Barnes and Company, 1947.

California Committee on Planning for Recreation, Park Areas and Facilities, R. L. Rathfon, Chairman. *Guide for Planning Recreation Parks in California,*

A Basis for Determining Local Recreation Space Standards, Documents Section, Printing Division, State of California, 1956.

Caplan, Frank. "The Playgrounds of Tomorrow," *Parks and Recreation*, 43:1 (January 1960), 18-19, 74.

Carmichael, Earl. "Make Your Parks People-Pleasers," *The American City* (April 1964), 104-106.

_____. "Park Plans Can Simplify Maintenance," *The American City* (October 1966), 104-106.

_____. "Santa Clara Provides New Areas, Facilities Through Bond Issue," *California Park and Recreation Quarterly* (September 1963), 8-9.

Church, Thomas D. *Gardens Are for People: How to Plan for Outdoor Living*. New York: Reinhold Publishing Corporation, 1955.

City of Santa Clara, Parks and Recreation Department. "Program of the Official Dedication of Central Park," 10 August 1974.

Connell, Edward Anthony. "What is a Good Public Park?" *Parks and Recreation*, 36:5 (May 1953), 5.

Contemporary Landscape Architecture and Its Sources. San Francisco Museum of Art, 1937.

Cranz, Galen. *The Politics of Park Design, A History of Urban Parks in America*. Cambridge, MA: MIT Press, 1982.

_____ and Michael Boland. "Defining the Sustainable Park: A Fifth Model for Urban Parks," *Landscape Journal*, 23: 2 (2004), 102-120.

Crawford, Robert W. "Recreation Programming, A Challenge," *Parks and Recreation*, 42:8 (August 1959), 378, 422-424.

Cutler, Phoebe. *The Public Landscape of the New Deal*. New Haven, CT: Yale University Press, 1985.

Dasmann, Raymond F. *The Destruction of California*. New York: The Macmillan Company, 1965.

"Designing Parks for Children," (anonymous), *Parks and Recreation*, 42, 6 (June 1959), 272-273, 281. An analysis of Royston's designs for Krusi Park and Mitchell Park. The illustrations of Mitchell Park are erroneous, since they depict the Rod and Gun Club.

"Designs for Play," (anonymous), *Recreation*, 52: 4 (April 1959), 130-131.

Doell, Charles E. "Park and Recreation People, An Attempt to Resolve Their Differences," *Parks and Recreation*, 42:7 (July 1959), 301-303, 324-325.

Eckbo, Garrett. *Landscape for Living*. An Architectural Record Book, F. W. Dodge Corporation, 1950.

_____. "Planning and Design Today," *Parks and Recreation*, 31:3 (March 1948), 99-105.

_____. *Public Landscape: Six Essays on Government and Environmental Design in the San Francisco Bay Area*. Institute of Governmental Studies, University of California Berkeley, 1978.

_____. *Urban Landscape Design*. New York: McGraw-Hill, 1964.

_____, Daniel U. Kiley, and James C. Rose. "Landscape Design in the Urban Environment," *Architectural Record*, 85:5 (May 1939), 70-77.

_____. "Landscape Design in the Rural Environment," *Architectural Record*, 86: 8 (August 1939), 68-74.

_____. "Landscape Design in the Primeval Environment," *Architectural Record*, 87: 2 (February 1940), 74-79.

Fein, Albert, ed. *Landscape into Cityscape, Frederick Law Olmsted's Plans for a Greater New York City*. Ithaca, N.Y.: Cornell University Press, 1967.

"For Employees: Relaxation in the Sun or the Shade," *Pacific Architect and Builder with Construction News Bulletin* (December 1957), 18-20.

French, Jere Stuart. *The California Garden and the Landscape Architects Who Shaped It*. Washington, D.C.: Landscape Architecture Foundation, 1993.

Gallion, Arthur B., and Simon Eisner. *The Urban Pattern, City Planning and Design*, second edition. New York: D. Van Nostrand Co., 1963.

Hartman, Chester. *The Transformation of San Francisco*. Totowa, NJ: Rowman and Allanheld Publishers, 1984.

Hogan, Elizabeth L., ed. *Parks of Palo Alto*. Palo Alto Historical Association, Palo Alto, California, 1996.

Howell, Edwin S. "Joint Use of Recreation Facilities by Cities, Counties and Schools," *Recreation*, 51:8 (October 1958), 286-287.

Hubbard, Henry V. "Parks and Playgrounds, Their Requirements and Distribution as Elements in the City Plan," *Landscape Architecture*, 12:4 (July 1922), 240-264.

_____. "The Size and Distribution of Playgrounds and Similar Recreation Facilities in American Cities," *Landscape Architecture*, 4:4 (July 1914), 133-144.

_____ and Theodora Kimball. *An Introduction to the Study of Landscape Design*. New York: The Macmillan Company, 1924.

Jackson, Kenneth T. *Crabgrass Frontier, The Suburbanization of the United States*. New York: Oxford University Press, 1985.

Johnson, Marilynn S. *The Second Gold Rush, Oakland and the East Bay in World War II*. Berkeley: University of California Press, 1993.

Kent, T. J., Jr. *The Urban General Plan*. San Francisco: Chandler Publishing Company, 1964.

Landscape Design. San Francisco Museum of Art and Association of Landscape Architects, San Francisco Region, 1948.

Laurie, Michael, with David Streatfield. *75 Years of Landscape Architecture at Berkeley, An Informal History, Part I: The First 50 Years*. Department of Landscape Architecture, University of California at Berkeley, 1988.

_____. *75 Years of Landscape Architecture at Berkeley, An Informal History, Part II: Recent Years*. Department of Landscape Architecture, University of California at Berkeley, 1992.

Ledermann, Alfred, and Alfred Trachsel, *Creative Playground and Recreation Centers*, New York: Frederick A. Praeger, 1959.

Lewis, Peirce F. "The Unprecedented City," *The American Land*, Smithsonian Exposition Books. New York: W. W. Norton and Company, 1979 (184-192).

Litton, R. Burton, Jr., ed. *Landscape Architecture 1958*. San Francisco Museum of Art, 1958.

Lynch, G. Leslie. "Design Recreation Areas ...Why?," *Recreation*, 52:3 (March 1959), 108-109.

Marx, Leo. *The Machine in the Garden, Technology and the Pastoral Ideal in America*. Oxford: Oxford University Press, 1964.

Moses, Robert. "Influence and Dominance of Parks," *Parks and Recreation*, 35:4 (April 1952), 29.

Mott, William Penn, Jr. "Changing Land Use Patterns," *Parks and Recreation*, 38: 5 (May 1955), 1.

_____. "Childrens' Fairyland," *Parks and Recreation*, 34:3 (March 1951), 5-7.

_____. "Magic Key to Your Park's Story," *Parks and Recreation*, 42:5 (May 1959), 220-221.

Neutra, Richard. "Index of Livability," *Sunset* (November 1943), 14-17.

Palo Alto Planning Commission. *Palo Alto General Plan*, 1963.

Palo Alto Planning Department. *Parks and Recreation Policy Study*, 1969.

_____. *Report on the Interim General Plan*, 1955.

"Palo Alto's Mitchell Park, A West Coast Design Leader," *The American City*, 72 (November 1957), 29.

Parks and Recreation Department, Santa Clara, California, Gold Medal Award Competition Application, 1966.

Perry, W. Allen. "Are Parks Here to Stay?" *Parks and Recreation*, 43:3 (March 1960), 130-131, 164-165.

Peterson, Stephanie M. "Revisiting Robert Royston's Mitchell Park." Web site: http://www.tclf.org/mitchell_park.htm

Pincetl, Stephanie S. *Transforming California, A Political History of Land Use and Development*. Baltimore: Johns Hopkins Press, 1999.

Playground and Recreation Association of America. *Play Areas: Their Design and Equipment*. New York: A. S. Barnes and Company, 1928.

Reid, Charles E. "National Recreation Trends," *Recreation*, 51:6 (September 1958), 254-256.

Rogers, Elizabeth Barlow. *Landscape Design: A Cultural and Architectural History*. New York: Harry N. Abrams, Inc., 2001.

Santa Clara County Planning Department. *A Plan of Regional Parks for Santa Clara County*, San Jose, 1972.

Santa Clara County Planning Commission. *A General Plan for Santa Clara County*. San Jose, 1960.

_____. *A Plan for Parks, Recreation and Open Space*. San Jose, 1959.

_____. *Neighborhood Standards for County Areas*, 1953.

Sayenian, Annalee. *Regional Advantage, Culture and Competition in Silicon Valley and Route 128*. Cambridge, MA: Harvard University Press, 1994.

Schuyler, David. *The New Urban Landscape: The Redefinition of Urban Form in Nineteenth-Century America*. Baltimore: Johns Hopkins University Press, 1986.

Scott, Mel. *The San Francisco Bay Area, A Metropolis in Perspective*, second edition. Berkeley: University of California Press, 1985.

Scott, Walter. "Planning Park and Recreation Areas," *Recreation*, 52:5 (May 1959), 196.

Shepherd, Harry W. "Design in Park Planting," *Parks and Recreation*, 24:10 (October 1941), 63-65.

Simo, Melanie Louise. "The Education of a Modern Landscape Designer," *Pacific Horticulture*, 49: 2

(Summer 1988), 19-30.

_____. *100 Years of Landscape Architecture: Some Patterns of a Century*. Washington, D.C.: ASLA Press, 1999.

Smith, Stanley L. "America's First Play Sculpture at Oakland," *Parks and Recreation*, 35: 7 (July 1952), 18-19.

Starr, Kevin. *The Dream Ends, California Enters the 1940s*. New York: Oxford University Press, 1997.

_____. *Endangered Dreams, The Great Depression in California*. New York: Oxford University Press, 1996.

_____. *Inventing the Dream, California Through the Progressive Era*. New York: Oxford University Press, 1985.

Streatfield, David C. *California Gardens: Creating a New Eden*. New York: Abbeville Press Publishers, 1994.

_____. "The Evolution of the California Landscape": Part 1, "Settling into Arcadia," *Landscape Architecture*, January 1976; Part 2, "Arcadia Compromised," March 1976; Part 3, "The Great Promotions," May 1977; Part 4, "Suburbia at the Zenith," September 1977.

Tilton, Leon Deming. *A Master Plan for Palo Alto, California*. Preliminary Draft. Palo Alto, 1949.

Treib, Marc, ed. *Modern Landscape Architecture: A Critical Review*. Cambridge, MA: MIT Press, 1993.

_____, ed. *Thomas Church Landscape Architect,*

Designing a Modern California Landscape. San Francisco: William Stout Publishers, 2003.

_____ and Dorothée Imbert. *Garrett Eckbo, Modern Landscapes for Living*. Berkeley: University of California Press, 1997.

Tritenbach, Paul. "Park Planning, More Than Meets the Eye," *Parks and Recreation*, 40:12 (December 1957), 4, 8-9, 17.

Twichell, Allan A., ed. *Planning the Neighborhood*, American Public Health Association Committee on the Hygiene of Housing, Public Administration Service. Chicago: R.R. Donnelley and Sons, Co., 1948.

Vance, James E., Jr. *Geography and Urban Evolution in the San Francisco Bay Area*. Institute of Governmental Studies, Berkeley, California, 1964.

Wallace, John J. "Robert Royston Landscape Architect," Unpublished master's thesis, University of California, Berkeley, 1992.

Weir, L. H. "Historical Background of Recreation in America," *Parks and Recreation*, 29:3 (July-August 1946), 238-243.

_____. "Leisure Time into Production," *Parks and Recreation*, 26:5 (May-June 1943), 206-208.

_____, ed. *Parks, A Manual of Municipal and County Parks*, 2 vols. New York: A. S. Barnes and Company, 1928.

Williams, Harold W. "Can Recreation Have an Ulterior Motive?," *Recreation*, 51:6 (September 1958), 228-229.

Wilsey and Ham, Engineers and Planners, *Report on a General Plan for the City of Santa Clara, California*, Millbrae, California, December 1959.

Wilson, Edward O. *Biophilia, The Human Bond with Other Species*. Cambridge, MA: Harvard University Press, 1984.

Wirth, Conrad L. "Basic Need for Land," *Parks and Recreation*, 40:11 (November 1957), 6, 18-20.

_____. "Parks Are for People," *Parks and Recreation*, 42:6 (June 1959), 262, 264-265.

Zaitzevsky, Cynthia. *Frederick Law Olmsted and the Boston Park System*. Cambridge, MA: The Belknap Press of Harvard University Press, 1982.

The Robert N. Royston/RHAA Collection

The Robert N. Royston/RHAA collection spans the years 1941-1990, with the bulk of the records dating from 1946-1976. The collection is organized into nine series: Professional Papers, Faculty Papers, Office Records, Project Records, and five Major Projects (Bay Area Rapid Transit/BART; California State University /Stanislaus College; San Joaquin Delta Junior College; University of California, San Francisco; and University of Utah).

The first three series are rather limited in their documentation. The Professional Papers contain primarily correspondence with other professionals and academics, materials from Royston's membership on the University of California, San Francisco Campus Planning Committee, mounted awards, and some lecture and reference notes. The Faculty Papers contain syllabi and student work from Royston's courses taught in the Department of Landscape Architecture at the University of California, Berkeley. The Office Records consist primarily of project photographs taken for promotional purposes.

In contrast, the Project Records series is extensive, documenting more than 2,000 projects—residential, civic, commercial, institutional, and industrial. The project files contain correspondence with clients, as well as budgets, punch and plant lists, project specifications, working drawings, and construction photographs. Within the Project Records, commissions initiated before 1965 are arranged alphabetically; projects begun after 1 January 1965 are arranged chronologically and by job number. Royston's collaborations with numerous architects including John Lyon Reid, Henry Hill, Claude Oakland, John Dinwiddie, Fred Langhorst, Mario Corbett, Worley Wong, William Wurster, Callister & Hillmer, and John Funk appear in the Project Records. Of particular interest are Royston's landscape designs for various subdivisions and individual houses built by Eichler Homes, T. Jack Foster and Sons (Foster City), and many FHA- and HUD-funded projects.

The records in the Major Projects series were prepared over a number of years and represent clients with whom Royston and his firm had extended working relationships. The original order of the files has been maintained. The Bay Area Rapid Transit/BART series includes correspondence, specifications, contract documents, and drawings relating to the design of the Richmond line and the El Cerrito, Berkeley, and Ashby stations. Correspondence and drawings also represent various projects for the California State University/Stanislaus College, the San Joaquin Delta Junior College, and the University of Utah. The University of California, San Francisco, series documents the long-range planning studies and other projects on the campus, particularly the School of Dentistry.

Other Environmental Design Archives collections with relevance to research on Robert Royston include the papers of Garrett Eckbo; John Funk; Henry Hill/Jack Kruse; Oakland & Imada; and George Rockrise.

Finding aids for the Robert N. Royston/ RHAA Collection may be previewed on the Environmental Design Archives' website:

http://www.ced.berkeley.edu/cedarchives and on the Online Archive of California: http://www.oac.cdlib.org/

Mailing Address

Environmental Design Archives
230 Wurster Hall #1820
University of California
Berkeley, CA 94720-1820

Office and Reading Room

280 Wurster Hall

Telephone: 510.642.5124
Fax: 510.642.2824
Email: designarchives@berkeley.edu
URL:http://www.ced.berkeley.edu/cedarchives

Index

Numbers in *italics* indicate
illustrations of the entries.